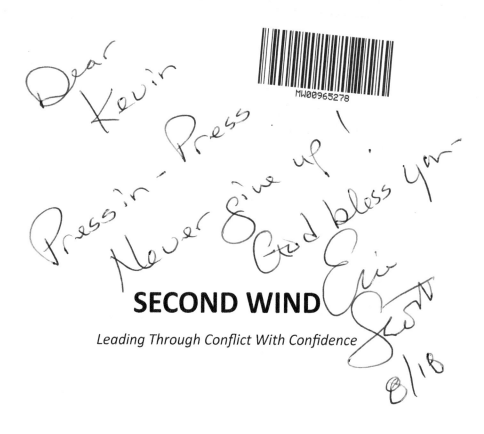

Dear Kevin

Pressin - Press

Never give up!

God bless you

Eric Scott

8/18

SECOND WIND

Leading Through Conflict With Confidence

By
DR. ERIC W. SCOTT

Xulon
PRESS

SECOND WIND
Leading Through Conflict With Confidence
by Dr. Eric W. Scott

Printed in the United States of America.

ISBN 9781545602614

www.xulonpress.com

ENDORSEMENTS

Second Wind is a breath of fresh air. Every now and then an excellent read comes my way, and Second Wind by Dr. Eric Scott is one of them. Dr. Eric has a keen way of weaving relevant Scripture with outstanding quotes from a variety of authors. His Second Wind principles at the end of each chapter, "read, reflect and reset" are insightful and helpful. I've known Dr. Eric to be a great preacher and teacher, but I'm thrilled to find that he is also a fantastic author. I enjoyed reading his book immensely, and I highly recommend it.

Rev. Dr. Ronald V. Burgio
President Emeritus, Elim Fellowship
Lead Pastor, Love Joy Church, Buffalo New York

Through the years I have encountered many talented people with exceptional skills who became leaders. It seemed like they were destined for great things, but as the years passed I began to wonder whatever happened to them. It seemed as though they were nowhere to be found. Sadly, after some research I discovered that some, even with their great talents, somewhere along the road had burned out and never accomplished their destiny. This is disturbing and should never happen.

In Dr. Eric W. Scott's new book "Second Wind," he gives practical advice on how to avoid burnout and lead with confidence even when there is conflict on all sides. His leadership principles are grounded in Scripture. When these principles are put into action, they will prevent the reader from experiencing fatigue and failure. Dr. Scott also gives insight on how to identify and train leaders within your sphere of influence. He asks the question, "Are you raising up followers or leaders?"

When the principles of this book are followed the entire organization will be strengthened. Beyond that, there will be no dissent or discord because the leaders have mastered good communication skills. In that environment, the whole group can know firsthand the truth of Psalm 133:1 where it says, "It is good and pleasant when brothers and sisters dwell together in unity."

This is an excellent book for the development of leaders in all settings.

Dr. Larry Ollison

President

International Convention of Faith Ministries

Anyone with a dream knows the anticipation of its fulfill-
ment – only to find themselves hitting a wall of exhaustion
and frustration. It is at that crucial point that we all need a
Second Wind.

Dr. Eric Scott's book provides clear, relevant and energizing principles empowering us to inhale Kingdom Air and
experience a fresh Divine surge that will propel us to victory.

This book is not abstract philosophy operating in some
mystical twilight zone, but clear systematic principles based
on Scripture that are embraceable and effective in our world.
As you read you will receive new strength and fresh wisdom
to be a Kingdom Achiever. You will be one who leads, lives
and serves with impact and influence.

Thank you, Dr Scott, for helping us catch our ***Second Wind***
and for causing us to see anew that ***The Future is Bright and
The Vision has Value!***

Dr. O. Mike Brown

Founder and President

Strength and Wisdom Ministries, Branson MO

FOREWORD

"O ver the river and through the woods" is a nostalgic tune sung during the Yuletide season. But for many, it describes the pathway to their purpose. I have witnessed the "rivers and woods" that Eric and Deby have traversed in their lifetime of effective ministry.

We first met in 1989 at the Elim Bible Institute and College where I served as Dean of Students and Instructor. At that time, Elim continued to feel the effects of the "Jesus Movement" especially from the West. They came sometimes straight from the commune on the West Coast. It was a challenge for a small town college in upstate New York to handle the influx of this counter-culture. But God, as always, was good and we all came through it together.

For this couple, just crossing the United States was a major step of faith. They knew no one in the area but were willing to "risk it" because of what they considered to be a call to ministry. From the beginning they were givers. They asked little and were willing to do whatever was required of them. They were focused, sacrificial and studious. They were always looking for opportunities to serve. Then just such an opportunity opened up in a small town not far away in the call for an assistant minister at a pioneer church. Nothing was offered to them except the opportunity to serve God and His people.

Through the years, they have shown their love for family by adopting six children, each one coming with their own challenges and needs. Eric and Deby embraced them all as they bonded into one loving family. This couple has the unique ability to juggle multi-ministries. Eric never allowed community or denominational limitations to stifle his desire to fulfill his calling. To this day he and Deby serve with a love for the world and a deep concern for their town and their region. Even during a season when he hit a ministry "glass ceiling" and was forced to re-evaluate his calling and direction, he was determined to honor the Lord and his fellow servants of God. Through that test of faith as well as many others, Eric and Deby have come out of the wilderness "in the power of the Holy Spirit."

I have also seen him in action, in Kenya and in India. He is self-motivated and able to adjust to new and different cultural demands. He asks little and gives much. He has committed himself to preaching and teaching in pastoral seminars and conferences in many nations. His Godly influence and life have been the example of a true servant.

Thousands of pastors have received his spiritual and some-times even financial assistance to make them stronger.

This book incorporates the principles of leadership within the context of spiritual service and is punctuated with a large dosage of humanity. Personal stories make this volume applicable to just about everybody. It will build your faith and encourage your heart. It is a must for leaders on any level. As I have known their journey, I have become stronger and more confident of God's awesome power at work in my own life.

May the warmth and wealth of this book bring a **Second Wind** to you, to your family and to your work. And may the sweet gentle rain of the Holy Spirit cultivate new growth and a fresh focus upon your destiny of care, leadership and progress in His kingdom here on earth.

Rev. Paul Johansson
President Emeritus Elim Bible Institute and College

DEDICATION

This book is dedicated, first and foremost, to the Lord Jesus Christ. Who, due to no strength, greatness or value on my part, chose of His own free will to love me, to save me and to change me. He took me from a life of doubt and worry and confusion into a new life flooded with grace, goodness, joy and peace. He is amazing and truly I am alive because of His intervention.

Second, only after God Himself, I devote these pages to Deby my wife. She has been and continues to be my companion, my friend, my confidant and my primary cheer leader for over forty years. She has believed in me even when I couldn't believe in myself. She is my joy and my heart's desire. Let's go for another forty – what do you say honey?

I can't finish without mentioning our seven children, our daughter-in-law and our two grand- daughters. You give us joy. You fill our world. We see hope and a positive future full of the promises of God for all of you. Our best days are still ahead.

Finally, I thank all the people of Celebrate! Family Church. Most of what I know has come from being among a people who love the Lord and love each other and who have taken the time to show me how to do the same. It is a joy and a privilege to serve the One True God alongside each one of you. May the blessing of the Lord follow you and overtake you, this day and every day.

TABLE OF CONTENTS

Introductory Thoughts xvii
     Why is there a Harley Davidson on the cover?

Chapter 1 – Just keep going 29
     Why we do what we do

Chapter 2 – Outward Growth 63
     Acts 6:1 "The church was multiplying…"

Chapter 3 – Inner Conflict 81
     Acts 6:1 "There arose a complaint…"

Chapter 4 – Openness to Change 97
     Acts 6:2 "…The twelve summoned…"

Chapter 5 – Local Leadership and Membership 121
     Acts 6:2 " (…the twelve) Summoned the
     multitude…"

Chapter 6 – Raising and Releasing Leaders 135
     Acts 6:3 "Seek out from among you…"

Chapter 7 – Focused Purpose 168
     Acts 6:4 "…We will give ourselves continually…"

Chapter 8 – Contentment 185
        Acts 6:5 "The saying pleased the
        whole group..."
Chapter 9 – Continued Blessing 202
        Acts 6:7 "...The word of God spread...
        the disciples multiplied greatly..." 213
Chapter 10 – Public Recognition. 213
        Acts 6:6 "...They laid hands on them..."
Chapter 11 – The Journey Continues 238
        The Future is Bright – The Value of Vision

Appendices. 251
Bibliography 263

INTRODUCTORY THOUGHTS

Why is there a Harley Davidson on the cover?

I have always loved motorized vehicles

Like most boys, I became interested in motorized vehicles when I was quite young. It started out with riding friends' mini-bikes and go-karts and progressed from there. When I was about twelve years old my brother and I got our hands on an old Porter-Cable riding lawn mower – you know, the ones with the big y-shaped yoke of tubular steel that looked like an old stroller handle for a steering bar. We stripped that thing down to its bare bones – a frame, a seat, wheels, a motor and the steering bar – I think it topped out at about seven miles per hour! We thought it was the best thing ever – we literally ran that mower until it just wouldn't go anymore! Then, we graduated to motorcycles. I was thirteen or fourteen when somehow I came into possession of a 1964 Honda 50 miniature motorcycle for a hundred dollars. We were in the big time then! I think our new ride maxxed out somewhere close to the speed of sound – probably about forty-five miles per hour! We modified it, put knobby tires on it, messed with the exhaust, fiddled with the carburetor – and it still only went forty-five miles an hour. Actually, we needed a good tail wind and a steep downhill to get it to a full forty-five, but we were thrilled nevertheless.

The crown jewel of motorcycles

Over the years, I've owned several different motorcycles. I've ridden Hondas, Kawasakis, Yamahas, Suzukis, Bultacos, BMW's you name it. If it had two wheels and I owned it, or could get whoever did own it to let me ride it – I was game to give it a try. But the piece-de-resistance – the crown jewel – in my motorcycling "career" came when the brother-in-law of a friend of mine in California came by my house one day with his Harley Davidson Electra Glide. And, get this, not only did he come by – he asked me if I'd like to take it for a ride! Had I been a religious man at the time and had I listened carefully, I'm sure I would have heard Handel's Hallelujah Chorus, sung by the heavenly host, in the background!

I rode that big, loud, black beauty that day! The owner took a few minutes to show me all the controls and to warn me that "it's really heavy" and not to lean it over too far. He showed me how to start it and explained how to shift my way through the gears. Then he backed away and said – "Go ahead, and take 'er for a spin".

My heart was settled, I was going to have one

I didn't go far, just a couple of times around the block, and then down the long main road that led to our little side street. But it was far enough! I was hooked – my heart was settled; I was going to have a big black Harley Davidson of my own. Somehow, some way, there WOULD be an Electra Glide parked in my driveway someday! I never forgot that passion. All I had to do was close my eyes, and with just a little dreaming, I could remember the sound and the feel of the power. The smooth acceleration and the feeling that I had enough steel beneath me to build a small tank was indelibly etched into my thinking. I dreamed of that Someday-Harley for almost three decades.

A Harley Davidson of my own!

Then in 2003 I came across a small Harley dealership in a town not far from my home. The people were personable, it wasn't too much of a drive AND they allowed me to test drive any bike I wanted! Can you guess what I chose? Right! A big black Electra Glide! Now I was double-hooked! I rode all the used bikes and inwardly drooled all over the new bikes. "But I have obligations. I have children. I pastor a church. What will people think? Where will I get the money?" I had many more questions than answers. But the dream wouldn't go away.

I found myself thinking of the passage from Ecclesiastes 5:3 in the Amplified Bible "...a dream comes with much business and painful effort..." and I concluded that if it was important and I prioritized its value, then the Lord would help me find a way! My wife was very supportive of my new "addiction." She even brought up the fact that up to that point I had been looking solely at used models. She also aptly noted that a new Harley at that time was only about two thousand dollars more than a used one. AND she pointed out that a new machine comes with a warranty and zero miles on the odometer. How about that! My wife talked me <u>into</u> looking for a new Harley Davidson! I'm not sure I need to say it, but I want everyone to know – I have an amazing wife!

I signed the line and set a delivery date

So, things led to things. I spoke with the owner of the shop whom I had come to know from my constant visits and test rides. She essentially echoed the sentiments of my wife, and before I knew it, I had committed to purchase a brand new, 2004 black Electra Glide. My dream would come to life as soon as the new models were released the following year. I gave her a few hundred dollars down, signed on the line and set a delivery date of June 2004 (about eight months from my order date). I walked out of the shop with twin emotions. First I thought – "this is the most incredible day of my life – I'm going to get a brand new Harley". Secondly I thought – "Oh brother, I've really bitten off a huge chunk this time!"

Practical preparation

The next eight months seemed to last forever. I saved more money and arranged financing for the remaining balance. I shopped for helmets and gloves and leathers. What was that Scripture? A dream comes with much business…? (Ecclesiastes 5:3 Amplified Bible) A lot of practical preparation went into the next few months but there was something else going on as well. I continued to have doubts about whether or not I could afford it. I was still concerned with what people would think about it. It got back to me that someone at the church had commented "If he can ride a Harley Davidson then that church doesn't need my money!" Not surprisingly, I later found that that person never gave anything to the church anyway!

"If that guy worked for me – he wouldn't be working for me"
(Harv Dykstra – Observing a worker with a bad attitude)

There are plenty of "wet blankets"

I learned early in my ministry that there are always more than enough "wet blankets" to go around. A "wet blanket" is someone who always voices a negative opinion. What we really need in the church today is a few folks who see someone on fire for God and filled with faith and excited about the gospel, and then, instead of tossing a wet blanket trying to shut the individual down, they throw a cup of gas on the fire. They're the ones who exclaim – "Atta boy – Atta girl – let's crank up the heat on this baby and see what our God can do!"

I got the bike!

So, long story short – I got the bike! The day I rode it home, grinning literally from ear to ear, I learned my first important biker lesson – keep your mouth closed unless you like the taste of bugs at sixty miles per hour! We rode it everywhere. I think we put in excess of 5000 miles on it that first summer. We got so much enjoyment out of the Electra Glide that a couple of years later my wife got her own Harley! In fact, her Harley is newer and has a bigger engine than mine! Who would have guessed? But the story doesn't end there and it's not all pretty.

I came to a place where I began to doubt everything

I wish I could say that all was well, that we lived happily ever after, and that we just rode off toward the sunset into motorcycle bliss. But storms lay ahead. Not too many years ago I reached a point in my life where I was just weary of the everyday grind. I'd had a few setbacks in ministry, I was feeling some financial pressure, I was working too many hours and I was just plain tired of the same old grind. The church had gone through some periods of financial challenge. We had a bunch of kids and that put us in various seasons of relational and financial struggle. I had a huge meltdown with some ministry friends that threw me into a three year-long tailspin of second-guessing everything from my call to gospel ministry, to the reasonability of a pastor riding a Harley Davidson. Over time I came to the place where I doubted every aspect of the things going on in my life. I had learned that I could always be confident in my wife and my God – but virtually EVERY other area of my life seemed to be in a state of flux.

We hit an emotional wall

That period of time in our lives felt dark and lonely and like there was no end in sight. I was tired all the time, I had no interest in anything. I had no energy. In my heart I felt like saying "What's the use?" "No matter what I do, it seems like I can't win." The wall we hit wasn't visible or tangible.

We hit an emotional wall that had spiritual and physical ramifications. We began to wear out mentally. Some call it "burn-out", others identify it as "bad attitude". Whatever you call it, we were feeling the crunch of life. I was tired and run down and desperately in need of some major changes in my life. I just wanted to quit everything. I was feeling like, "OK world, I'm done – forget the dream – you win, I quit!" It was a dark and difficult time for us.

Then, one day, out of nowhere, I got the idea, "let's just sell the bikes". Right now you might be thinking, "so big deal – selling a motorcycle – why is that news?" It's because the bikes represented our freedom to dream! They symbolized, to us anyway, new days and fresh adventures and uncharted possibilities for our lives. The bikes in themselves are no big deal, but their value is far more than money or two-wheeled metal in our lives. Those bikes had given us hundreds of hours of enjoyment. Too many times to count, the bikes had been the catalyst for Deby and I to just be together – no cell phones, no computers, no office hours. Just us and the open road – the wind in our hair and an untapped horizon waiting just over the next rise. We loved our time together on those big bikes. We thought, we prayed, we dreamt, we relaxed. Getting rid of them was my emotionally broken way of concluding that it was no use trying to go on – in vision, in destiny or in ministry. I was ready to give up.

"Stay with God! Take heart. Don't quit."
(Psalm 27:14 – The Message)

"You need to change the way you're doing life"

During this time, through a ministry acquaintance, I encountered a friend, Dr. Keith Johnson. He had the courage to tell me what I really needed to hear. He said, "go ahead and sell the bikes if you want, but it's not going to change anything." "What – Didn't you hear what I just said? I'm burned man, I'm tired out and I'm worn thin!" But Keith went on – "You need to change the way you're doing life, not the way you ride a motorcycle!" Cold shower! Wake-up call! Attitude adjustment! That interaction caused me to re-think my values and my priorities. It focused my attention on my heart, my destiny, my calling and my future. My problem wasn't a motorcycle!

The Harley reminds me that the dream is worth the effort

My problem was that I had lost my fire, lost my vision – I had let the "tyranny of the urgent" rob me of quality time and energy and faith and confidence to continue in the pursuit of my purpose for being on the planet. Sure the dream comes with much struggle, there may even be pain involved – but the dream – my dream – your dream – is worth the effort! As a result of that challenge from a courageous friend on a dark, cold and wet northern New York autumn day, I came face to face with my own SECOND WIND. And in case you're wondering, we still have the Harleys and we ride them every chance we get!

Now is the time!

I love the passage from Second Corinthians "...**now** is the accepted time; behold, **now** is the day of salvation..." (2 Corinthians 6:2). We would most likely, in today's vernacular, say "today is the day". But the apostle wasn't looking at days, he was looking at moments in time. An old farmer asked "What's the best time to plant an oak tree?" The answer is simple, "Thirty years ago!" Then the farmer asked part two of his question – "What's the second best time to plant an oak tree?" The answer again is simple – "Do it today!"

"I'm not on my way down and out –
I'm on my way up and over!"
(Rev. Tim Gilligan)

It's your turn!

Why share all of this? Because God has a plan for me and He has a plan for you. Whether you are growing a family, a church, a business or just want to grow yourself – a Mighty God is in the midst of your life. He knows you and He wants you to know Him — He wants to help you, He wants to care for you, advise you, guide you and love you — Why share all of this? Because it's your turn — Now the Lord wants to make sure that you get your Second Wind!

Second Wind Principles

At the end of each chapter I have included a brief personal feed-back section called "Second Wind Principles". Each section will include three steps for application: "Read" — "Reflect" — "Reset". Do yourself a favor by taking a few moments to consider the previous chapter. Then seek the Lord and what He is saying about your Second Wind. Start right now with "Second Wind Session" #1:

Read:

> ...He leads me beside the still waters.
> 3 He restores my soul... (Psalms 23:2-3)

Reflect:

The "23rd Psalm" has become a staple of most memorial services. I'm not really sure why a story of the assurance of God's love, care and provision has been co-opted as the funeral reading of choice. Look at all the promises: He is "my shepherd" or he is the ultimate caregiver, even laying down

His own life for His "charges" us (John 10:11)! "I will not want" or I will lack nothing. He makes me, or causes me, or gives me an opportunity, to rest while under His complete care and protection (v.2). He takes me to the "still" (good, healthy, quiet, restorative) waters – keeping watch over me the whole time. He leads me and gives me His righteousness (right standing before the Father). Even in the face of death (or seriously difficult life), Lord I will not fear – because You are always there with Your care, Your protection and Your comfort.

Reset:

1   What does a "Second Wind" in your life look like?

———————————————————————

2   How has God taken care of you in the past?

———————————————————————

3   What would you like to see Him do for you in the future?

———————————————————————

4   What area(s) can you submit to Him for even more protection and growth?

———————————————————————

Chapter 1

JUST KEEP GOING

Why we do what we do

In the Disney movie "Finding Nemo" Dory asks Marlin – "When life gets you down, do you know what you've gotta do?" Dory's answer to the challenges life throws at us has become world-famous – "Just keep swimming, just keep swimming…" Real life, it seems, often comes down to living out that so-simple, yet so profound advice…No matter what you are facing, don't quit swimming. Just keep going!

A long-time friend of mine runs marathons. I so envy her and her determination, not to mention her health and vitality. Several years ago, she was relating what the preparation regimen is like when she is planning for a marathon. I hadn't realized the level of commitment and the amount of effort that goes into a long distance run. I was particularly surprised by the length of time spent in daily training. I was unaware that she begins her preparation 6 months to a year ahead of the race! Her routine covers diet, sleep, mental toughness, and of course physical training – lots of physical training.

Hitting the wall

When I asked about the mental toughness aspect of running she got a serious look on her face. She explained that this had been one of her biggest obstacles. She further enlightened my understanding by recounting a particular aspect of running. She called it "hitting the wall," and revealed that every time she runs more than a few miles she always experiences "the wall". Every time, no exceptions. My friend elaborated that when an athlete hits the wall, it's not a literal wall, but a mental monolith that tells them – "this is it, you're done, you're not going to make it, you've got to quit – NOW!" My friend said that at her current experience level she's aware and ready for this phenomenon; but early-on, when she first started running, she was caught completely off-guard. In fact, the first few times it happened she quit running thinking she was having some kind of insurmountable physical shut-down. Then I saw this little grin on her face as she said "but I've got it figured out now". I had to know. "What do you do differently now? What do you do when you hit the wall these days?" Again, that sheepish little grin as she nonchalantly informed me – "Oh, I just keep going!" Then she gave me my title for this work – she said "after the wall, I get my SECOND WIND and then I can run for miles and miles".

"Lead, Follow or Get out of the way"
(General George Patton)

There have always been struggles!

When I assumed my responsibilities as Senior Pastor over two decades ago I thought I was ready for anything. Bible College had equipped me for everything from demonology to marriage counseling. I was ready for "the world, the flesh and the devil," but I was not prepared for the everyday challenges of leading the world's largest group of volunteers – the Local Church. The struggles of the church in general and the suspicion that "something must be wrong with my church" (or is it me?) are linked to the idea that things could be, should be, used to be different. The assumption that our current problems, struggles and issues are new or exclusive to us or to our group or some denomination or a specific location fails to take into consideration much of the Biblical narrative. Biblically speaking, there have always been struggles.

Adam and Eve blew it

Adam and Eve blew it and we've been dealing with the consequences ever since! Noah had to face continual rejection and hostility while working non-stop for a hundred years to build the Ark by himself. Moses had to deal with getting a million-plus people past a raging sea while seeing the dust-cloud of an angry army in hot pursuit over his shoulder. Joshua had to figure out who took the forbidden items during the raid on Jericho thus causing the abysmal failure of the army at Ai. He was ultimately required by God to proctor the elimination of an entire family from his "church membership" for their sin (Joshua 7:25). These and many other challenges have dogged the people of God. The struggle continues all the way into the New Testament. There we see Peter standing helplessly by as Ananias and Sapphira lied to and were subsequently annihilated by the Holy Spirit for pretending to be "all-in." It was a sad and misguided attempt to mislead the congregation while simultaneously misrepresenting themselves (Acts 5:6). Fast-forward to our world, and we find that the challenges and struggles of those days are still very much alive and active in this current day of Kingdom advance.

The rewards outweigh the challenges

Granted, the experiences previously cited are extreme and unusual and it is highly unlikely that any of us will ever see them reproduced during any ministry we will be involved in. Regardless of the unlikelihood that any of these former events will ever be repeated, the examples do serve to raise our awareness to the fact that human nature has not changed much (at all?) since that first sin in the garden. Difficulty and struggle have always surrounded the forward advance of the Kingdom of God. Yet every generation from then until now has come to the conclusion that the rewards of following Him far outweigh the challenges and costs associated with that pursuit.

"I often go to sleep with an insoluble problem –
When I awake the answer is there"
(George Washington Carver)

Some have considered "throwing in the towel"

In over twenty years of serving others in various roles of pastoral and apostolic oversight, I have been dismayed at how many ministers feel insecure and inadequate in their calling and service. I have personally felt on many occasions that quitting the ministry all together would be easier and more advantageous to everyone than continuing the work. The problems, the personal attacks, the lack of commitment, the financial struggles, to name a few of the issues, take their toll on the leader (and the church member) to the degree that "throwing in the towel" seems like a viable solution.

Statistically Speaking:

- 80% of ministers believe that pastoral ministry negatively affects their families.
- 33% believe that ministry is an outright hazard to family life.
- 75% report having a significant stress-related crisis at least once in their ministry.
- 50% feel unable to meet the needs of the job.
- 90% feel inadequately trained to cope with ministry demands.
- 25% of pastors' wives see their husband's work schedule as a source of conflict.
- The clergy has the second highest divorce rate among all professions.
- 80% of pastors say they have insufficient time with their spouse.
- 56% of pastors' wives say that they have no close friends.
- 45% of pastors' wives say the greatest danger to themselves and their family is physical, emotional, mental and spiritual exhaustion.
- 52% of pastors say that being in ministry is hazardous to their family's well-being
- 45% of pastors say they have experienced depression or burnout

- 70% do not have someone they consider a close friend.[1]

The Number One reason given by pastors who leave the ministry is that church people are not willing to work in concert with the goals of the pastor. Pastors believe God wants them to go in one direction but the people are not willing to follow or change.[2]

Feelings of discouragement and personal struggle are normal

A perusal of Scripture shows that from a human perspective, feelings of discouragement and personal struggle are more the norm of ministry than the exception. Just consider the lives of Abraham, Moses and Peter. Abraham had been promised a child, but at almost 100 years of age and still childless, he begins to give in to discouragement. Moses is called and anointed by God to lead over a million Israelites out of captivity: he has overseen plagues, miracles and amazing escapes only to have his "flock" lament against him "If only we could return to Egypt". Peter has given up his livelihood, left his business and put all of his time and effort

---

[1] London, H.B. Jr. and Neil B. Wiseman; "Pastors at greater risk"; Regal Books, 2003; pp. 20, 86, 118, 148, 172, 264

[2] Statistics provided by The Fuller Institute, George Barna, and Pastoral Care Inc. 2015

into following and serving the newly revealed Messiah only to have his sense of self-worth dashed by his own fears and failures in the face of challenge. Even Jesus at one point in the Garden of Gethsemane queried His Heavenly Father "if You are willing... take this cup of suffering away from Me" (Luke 22:42 NLT). With these historic realities in mind, one is forced to reject the "quitting option" and begin to look for the overcoming possibilities provided by adherence to the Word of Truth and the empowerment of the Holy Spirit.

> *"There are three requirements of ministry:*
> *The heart of a child – The mind of a scholar –*
> *The hide of a rhinoceros!"*
> (Anonymous)

We expect to be "different"

The feelings of resentment, frustration and sometimes downright anger experienced by leaders are real and at times justifiable, but for the most part they are born out of misunderstanding. Unrealistic expectations are a large part of the pastoral dilemma; we expect the church or at least the people of the church to "be different". Different from the world around us, more understanding of faults and failures, more willing to give, to serve, to forgive. What we find is that people are people, human nature is what it is. Christians get angry. Church members get dissatisfied. Elders can have sin issues. Pastors have problems at home. So the "cry" goes up – "This is the church? We're supposed to be different!" The desired "difference" is a valid expectation and an admirable goal, but for the most part, it is a difficult, long-term and often elusive pursuit.

We can learn from the First Century

Most of the conclusions of this work are drawn from The Book of Acts – Chapter Six. This section of the Bible highlights the fantastic growth of the early church. People are being converted by the thousands. Lives are being changed. Healing is occurring. Giving is practiced. Leaders are being raised up and released. Churches are being planted. Missionaries are taking the faith to new regions. It's all good, right? Look again:

> "...in those days when the number of disciples was
> multiplying, *there arose a complaint...*"
> (Acts 6:1a Emphases added)

In the best days we can imagine for church growth and development – when everything was amazing and the fresh promise of the gospel was being promoted everywhere – a "complaint" surfaced and threatened the unity, harmony and integrity of the ministry.

I contend that the first century idiosyncrasies seen in Acts 6 are still the basis of many of our struggles today. Challenges in the ministry are manifold and *"normal"*! The Acts 6 passage goes on to enumerate the many issues they faced. Then we get to see the assessments the leaders made, the conclusions they drew and the action steps they took to address those needs. In the midst of the challenge, they continued to learn and to grow thereby accomplishing the work of the ministry assigned to them.

I further contend that our current-day failure to accept struggle as a "good" part of church life has led to many premature resignations by both clergy and laity. Our misinformed expectations, coupled with our failure to realistically review and apply our own church history, has been used by the enemy of our souls to discourage, anger and sometimes destroy churches, church members and church leaders.

"...We will harvest a good crop if we don't give up or quit..."
(Galatians 6:9 – The Message")

Finding fresh motivation to become...

Someone once said "forewarned is forearmed". The expression speaks to the value of personal awareness and preparation. It is hoped that the reflections proposed herein will serve to enlighten and prepare the reader for some of the struggles that arise in the course of "doing church".

Furthermore, the study will help all of us, laity and clergy alike, come to the realization that the "Normal Church" has always had, and will always have, its good and not-so-good moments. In addition to the history and the insights drawn from Acts 6, it is expected that the modern day Christian will herein find fresh motivation to become a problem-solver and a spiritual innovator. The ultimate outcome, of course, will be a renewed ability and a rekindled desire to address our current day struggles and to continue to cultivate and grow the Kingdom of God.

Seeing ourselves within history (His – Story)

This study will offer observations of the early church and its challenges, then relate those considerations to the issues facing modern-day church members and leaders. By seeing ourselves within the scope of history, we will find patience and determination, not to quit, but to press forward. We will seek new possibilities and fresh methods for our own Kingdom service. Our leadership skills will grow. And, as we continue to move ahead, we will find our own "Second Wind".

Have I got a deal for you

Since you're still reading I think I might know some things about you. Either, #1 you thought it was a catchy title and are just trying to figure out what it's about. Or, #2 you are feeling pushed around by your world, your life, your job, your church, or some other aspect of everyday coming and going. And/or #3 having been pushed around a little by the world out there, you're wondering if a "Second Wind" might be just the prescription your life needs right now. If your rationale for reading so far is #1 then I hope you'll stay with us and see what you can glean. If you're dealing with #2 or #3 then, as they say in New York City – "Have I got a deal for you"!

Why I quote the Bible

As we move forward together you may begin to wonder why I continually quote the Bible. I read and recite the Bible because I have discovered within its pages an incredible amount of wisdom, grace, love and down to earth, good, solid direction for everyday living.

"All Scripture is God-breathed and is useful for teaching, rebuking, correcting and training in righteousness, so that the man of God may be thoroughly equipped for every good work." (2 Timothy 3:16-17 NIV)

The Bible never wears out

Simply put, Second Timothy means that the advice, the standards and the directions of the Bible never wear out. They are never out of style. They are never not true or not applicable. The Bible is even more vital to "Kingdom

People" who are embracing a plan to be life-long learners and teachable teachers. To be a good leader one must first learn to be a good, dedicated, and loyal follower. It has been said that "you teach what you know, you reproduce what you are" (Wayne Cordiero). In a conversation with Rev. Carlton Spencer, son of the founder of Elim Bible Institute in northern central New York, he remarked with delight and with a sparkle in his eyes that he had been learning multiple, fresh insights from the Lord in recent days. I just listened and thought to myself – "I want to be this guy". You see, Rev. Spencer was already past ninety years of age at the time of that discussion! I want to be that excited about the Word of God when I'm ninety years old! Why quote the Bible? To learn, to grow, to have my thinking corrected, and to have my life, my family and my work enhanced. I want to be lifted and raised and released to new levels of personal and spiritual growth. I use the Bible and quote it often, because I have found that I never go wrong when I live by its words.

A look at The Book of Acts

So, with those things in mind, let's take a look at The Book of Acts.

> Now in those days, when the number of the disciples was multiplying, there arose a complaint against the Hebrews by the Hellenists,

because their widows were neglected in the daily distribution. Then the twelve summoned the multitude of the disciples and said, "It is not desirable that we should leave the word of God and serve tables. Therefore, brethren, seek out from among you seven men of good reputation, full of the Holy Spirit and wisdom, whom we may appoint over this business; but we will give ourselves continually to prayer and to the ministry of the word."

And the saying pleased the whole multitude. And they chose Stephen, a man full of faith and the Holy Spirit, and Philip, Prochorus, Nicanor, Timon, Parmenas, and Nicolas, a proselyte from Antioch, whom they set before the apostles; and when they had prayed, they laid hands on them.

Then the word of God spread, and the number of the disciples multiplied greatly in Jerusalem, and a great many of the priests were obedient to the faith. (Acts 6:1-7)

In those days...

Acts 6:1 "Now in those days..." In what days? What is Luke (the author) talking about?

The Book of Acts spans about forty years. Acts Chapter 6 occurs during the first year of the church's existence. Up to that point in church history the people of *"those days"* have seen the day turn to night at about noon on the day of Christ's crucifixion (Matthew 15:33). They've seen tombs opened, and formerly dead people up and walking around (Matthew 27:52). They've seen the blind healed, the lame walk, the deaf hear and the dead raised. They've seen the Holy Spirit poured out in a miraculous manifestation resulting in their having been accused of being drunk at 9 o'clock in the morning (Acts 2:4-13). In "those days" they witnessed the deaths of Ananias and Saphira when the couple attempted to deceive the Holy Spirit and the church (Acts 5:3ff). In "those" same days Saul had begun pursuing and persecuting "any who were of the Way whether men or women" (Acts 8:1; 9:1). They were great days, they were terrifying days, they were landmark and pacesetting days. The church was surging forward while the world around her offered resistance. First century life was pushing back against the gospel and the forward movement of the church.

"Leadership and learning are indispensable to one another"
(President John F. Kennedy)

43

Counteracting pressure

Traditionally, when the world squeezes or pushes the church, the church will push back. While the method of church push-back is not physical, it is usually tactical. The church counteracts pressure from without by strengthening from within. And with that strength comes new anointing and a re-doubling of her external efforts. That strategy is highlighted when Saul, who had "consented" to the death of Stephen (Acts 8:1) and was "breathing out threats and murder," (Acts 9:1) was knocked from his horse while on the road to Damascus (Acts 9:3-4). The remainder of the New Testament is filled with the story of how God changed Paul's heart and used him to spread the gospel throughout what would one day become the sub-continent of Europe.

The push-back from the hostility faced by the church was not a "fight force with force" scenario. Heaven "fights back" by an increase in the manifestation of the power of God. Demonic demonstration is overwhelmed by the dynamic authority of a life lived with and for God. Look at the immediate outcome of Stephen's death: "Philip went to Samaria and preached Christ...multitudes heeded the things spoken (by him)... hearing and seeing the miracles... unclean spirits came out...many paralyzed and lame were healed...And there was great joy" (Acts 8:4-8). Not exactly the response one might expect from a move of oppression upon a group of people. Instead of physical resistance, the church learned to "overcome evil with good" (Romans 12:21)

The concept of "Kingdom push-back"

The push-back in the Book of Acts is different from that found in corporate America. It's not self-defense against a bully. It's not an armed response to a rogue nation or an unwelcome intruder. This push-back is rooted in God's power. It is punctuated with God's grace. The push back I'm talking about is ordained and supported by Holy anointing. This is "Kingdom Push Back". When the Kingdom of God "suffers violence" (i.e. getting pushed) "violent (determined, courageous, devoted) men", women and children "take it by force" (Matthew 11:12). They push back by moving forward. They get smarter. They get better informed about the ways of the world, the ways of their enemy, and especially about the ways of their God.

We're not talking about carnal satisfaction, the sense of accomplishment that comes from winning an argument or proving a point. This is deeper. This is the joy that comes from relying upon God and seeing Him "show up". This is the peace and confidence found only as we rest in His authority and the certainty that His provision is "enough and too much" (Exodus 36:7 NIV). The power, the presence and the possibilities of the Acts 6 world are still available and effective for our lives today. It is my intention to ignite you to bring your own brand of "Kingdom Push Back" to the world you live in.

Have you ever hit the wall?

So, has it happened to you yet? Have you hit the wall? I know you've at least visited the wall a time or two! It happens to everybody. So many things are going on and you're like the juggler at the circus keeping all the plates spinning and all the balls in the air...and then it happens! An unforeseen mutiny among some close associates, a bad report from a doctor or your child's school counselor, a serious issue in the life of a family member or a good friend. One of the tellers at a bank I once used had a sign on her desk – "I know Mondays only come once a week, but lately I feel like several of them have hit me all at once." So I ask again, have you been to the wall yet?

From marriage to ministry to multiplication

Let me close this chapter by sharing some insight into my own personal life and history. First, I'd like to start out by saying – I have an amazing wife! Deby and I met in 1975 when we were both twenty years old. At that time, we were stationed together with the United States Air Force in Spokane, Washington. Deby is from southern California, I'm from upstate New York; we met in the state of Washington!

What are the odds? I have an amazing wife AND I have an amazing God!

We were both assigned to the medical services squadron of the Air Force and were introduced when we happened across one another in the dining hall of the hospital at the base. Honestly, I don't think she gave me much of a second look; but in retrospect, I can say from my side of the relationship, that it was love at first sight. Somehow, from the first time we met, way down deep inside, I sensed that this was going to be more than a casual connection.

We had a lot of fun getting to know each other. Suddenly everything seemed interesting. Even serving together at the hospital had a new intrigue attached to it. Excitement and joy seemed to surround my life. I found myself looking for excuses to walk by her office just to see if she was in, or maybe she could spare a few minutes to grab a cup of coffee. We dated, went hiking and camping and enjoyed four-wheeling in my roommates' Jeep. Her car broke down and I undertook the repairs. My apartment was a mess (three single military guys!) and she came over and "made" us clean it up! We were friends, we grew close, we fell in love.

We had love...but not much else

Deby and I were married in November of 1977 at a little Lutheran Church in Yorba Linda, California. Although we were married in a church, neither one of us was following the Lord.

We discovered the hard way that love and common interests could get us started on our life together, but it would require a stronger "glue" than that to cement our relationship and set us up to meet the rigors and demands of "real world" living.

We moved to southern California in early 1978 where I took a job as a carpenter's apprentice and Deby went to work in the office of a local contractor. It's a good thing that we had love, because we didn't have much of anything else. We didn't even have a refrigerator! We had tried to buy a fridge on credit from a local department store but we were declined because we'd been in the military for four years and had no credit record. We didn't have a bad credit record. We had NO credit record – we didn't even show up in any of the credit reporting agencies. We lived out of a Coleman cooler for months while we saved money for a refrigerator. Some people stop by the store for groceries every day, we stopped to buy ice for the cooler every day. All for love!

Married singles

Time went on, we finally got a fridge – a used one from somebody's garage for fifty bucks – but hey, it worked. And no more buying ice everyday – Life was good. I should say that from the outside it *looked like* life was good. The inside, though, told a different story. Our relationship, over time, had become strained. I drank beer, came home late and hung out with my friends more and more. My absenteeism (for the most part I was mentally, emotionally and relationally absent even when I was home) led to Deby spending more and more time with her mom and other family members. We became "married singles." We shared a home, we ate meals together (sometimes), we even shared a bed – however, relationally speaking; "the lights were on but nobody was home". We were physically present but we were relational no-shows. I mentioned earlier that during this time neither of us were pursuing nor following the Lord – but I am absolutely certain that He was pursuing and following us!

A new addition and a major wake-up call

In 1982 after five years of childlessness, many doctors and multiple lab tests (all of which resulted in the same medical conclusion – "I'm sorry but you will not be able to have children") – the Lord in His amazing grace saw fit to place a new addition in our household. He blessed us with a child by adoption. A little girl! We were elated – especially Deby.

Without going into all the details, we discovered within a few months that our baby had been severely malnourished as a tiny infant resulting in serious mental and physical limitations. But we didn't let that stop us. We loved her (and still do 34 years later!) and we have seen her beat the odds time and again with continual growth and developing abilities. The doctors said she wouldn't walk – she runs and rides a two-wheel bike! They said she wouldn't talk – we find that we sometimes wish we could get her to stop talking! She has a phone, she texts, she uses the internet, she can do math and count money and she works five days a week! Wow, what a God!

But even after the blessing of our little girl, I was still out on a regular basis until all hours of the day and night, drinking, partying and generally carrying on. This continued for roughly seven years. Then, one day I came home early from work and got a MAJOR wake-up call. It was an intervention by God that has changed our lives forever. As I walked through the front door into our home that day, I immediately sensed that something about the house was a little different. Actually, that's an understatement – what I found was that the house had been pretty much cleaned out! Pictures were missing, all of Deby's clothes were gone, most of our daughter's clothing, bedding, car seat and assorted baby paraphernalia – all gone! I was shocked! What happened? Were we robbed? But who steals a bunch of baby stuff and leaves the stereo and the television behind? I guess I'm not always the quickest guy on the uptake!

What have I done?

It took a few moments to register but then I realized – she was gone. They were gone. I found a note on the counter that confirmed my suspicions. The note said in effect – "I can't do this anymore – I love you but I don't like you or what you've become – I've taken the baby and moved, you can have the house." You know, when you take the family out of a home it becomes just a house! Its wood and plaster and carpet and just really empty and lonely and quiet. Very quiet. The question went through my mind "what have I done?"

I don't know why I'd never listened to her when she tried to explain her feelings. She felt like we were drifting apart. She couldn't understand why I'd say I was on my way home and then I'd show up four hours later or maybe not at all. She didn't know what to say to the neighbors or her family or my parents. What happened? How did we get into this mess?

God if You're real – I need You!

Although I hadn't listened before – I can tell you, on that day, in mid-October of 1985 – I was listening! She had my attention. But now she was gone. My baby was gone. My life was a mess. And it was all my own doing. I remember that day so clearly. It was a nice day outside my door, but it was dark and gloomy and lonely on the inside of the house.

Let me back track for just a moment. A few months before this dark day, my sister had contacted me from Colorado and was all excited about "what God had done" in her life. I remember that at that time I thought that she was a couple of two by four's short of a full load. She started telling me how a person could "get saved". She said I could know if I was going to heaven or not – I argued with her – "no one can know what happens after they die – you just die and then whatever happens, happens!" It seemed too far-fetched to be for real.

But on that day in October – the day my life was flooded with the darkness of lost relationship, broken hearts and shattered dreams – I remembered that conversation with my sister. In a moment of abject lostness, hurt, anxiety and guilt, I cried out in my living room "God IF you're real – I need you to do for me what you did for my sister!" Let me say this – if you ever think about praying a prayer like that – you'd better buckle your seat belt first!

"Everything will be alright"

In an instant and without warning I collapsed, landing on my face on the living room carpet. I felt cool wind blowing in my face. Lying on the floor, feeling wind in my face in a closed house with no heating or air conditioning turned on, I began "hearing" a voice. To this day it seems like it was in my own heart and head, but I just can't be sure. The voice was saying "I'm here my son – everything is going to be alright". Paul makes the statement that, at one point in his life, he had an experience "whether in the body or out of the body" he did not know (2Corinthians 12:3). My time in the living room was like that! Did it really happen? Was it real wind? Was it a real voice? If so, where did it come from? Whose voice was it? I looked around to double check; there was no one (visible) in my house.

By this time, I'm just lying on the living floor alternately sobbing and laughing. I remember saying out loud – "Oh great! Now I'm going to need a psychiatrist!" Had I lost my mind? I'd heard it said that too much partying could lead to hallucinations and even a mental break down. Was I losing it?

I'm not sure how long this experience lasted – I do know that when I got up, I felt like I was tingling from head to foot. I was wide awake – there was no hint of the hangover that had caused me to leave work and head home early – I was changed. I was different. I was brand new.

I jumped in my truck and drove to my wife's work – if she could just know what was going on, then she would come home and we could resume life.

But, hold it, not so fast! She said "I've heard all of your lies before – how many times have you promised that you're going to change and things will all be different?" Not only didn't she relent and say she'd come home, she told me that I had five minutes to get out of her office and off company property or she was going to call security! Hmmm – this was not going well at all.

A major turn

As I was walking down the hallway to the exit I remembered that a friend of mine had begun attending church and had told me about it a month or two earlier. I left Deby's work and went to my friend's shop. The more I shared of the experiences in my living room the more nervous he got! Voices? Wind? Laughing and crying? I think even he thought I was losing it! My friend considered my report for a few minutes, then he said "I know a minister who lives right around the corner from your house – go talk to him."

So that's exactly what I did! I showed up at the minister's house unknown, uninvited, unannounced and with a wild story to tell. Little did I know that my life was about to take a major turn. I shared my whole story with the pastor – the partying, the marriage, Deby's leaving, the voices, the laughing, the crying, my sister, inviting God – the whole deal. He got real excited and seemed genuinely interested – I was kind of shocked that he cared so much. I said "I don't even know what has happened to me." He leaned forward smiling and said – "You got saved! That's what happened!" I remember looking straight at him and asking "I did? Is that good?" "Oh", he said, "That's very good!"

I didn't even recognize myself!

It seems funny to write about all of this. I've told this story many times but I've never before written it down. As I write, it's all flooding back into my heart and mind. I can see the living room, feel the wind, I even hear the voice (yes

He is still speaking to me!). Let me tell you how that month turned out and then I'll explain why I've shared all of this.

During my meeting with the pastor he expressed an interest in meeting with Deby and I to help us work things out. I explained that I thought he was pretty much wasting his time as she had made it abundantly clear that there was NO WAY she was giving me another chance – I'm not talking about a second chance here – it was more like a fiftieth or eightieth "second chance." In any case, he somehow convinced Deby to join a meeting with me, the pastor and the pastor's wife. And somehow he convinced her that something major had happened to me – something like nothing either of us had ever known before – and that another "second chance" was worth a try.

Dear reader, I'm telling you – my life was so different, even I didn't recognize myself! Guys at work were saying "What has happened to you?" I never had another problem with drinking or drugs or any party behavior. I was healed of all addiction and any desire to participate in that lifestyle (or is it a death-style?) ever again – that deliverance is still in effect today more than thirty years later! Did I mention that I have a great wife AND I have a great God?

"I would have lost heart unless I had believed that I would see the goodness of God in the land of the living"
(Psalm 27:13)

Things were about to get real interesting

After about five days of my coming home early every day, playing with the baby, bringing my wife flowers, helping around the house, going on picnics down at the lake and generally acting like a normal married guy – Deby and I had a massive encounter with each other and the Lord. We were soon to discover that God can make life really interesting when we let Him in. I had arrived home from work ahead of her one day thinking to myself "this seems like a good time to bake some cookies for Deby and the baby." I mean, that in itself was news! I just didn't do stuff like that. So Deby comes in from work and I'm in an apron in the kitchen, up to my elbows in flour, humming and whistling and just being happy and alive and totally sober – and feeling like life was really good. Deby walks in and takes one look at me and raises her voice – "STOP!" – she says. I looked at her with wonder and said "What's the matter?" To which she exclaimed – "WHAT ARE YOU DOING?" and to which I responded "I'm baking cookies, what does it look like?"

What has happened to you?

At that moment she steps really close, grabs both of my wrists and looks me in the eye saying – "What has happened to you?" I said, "I don't really know, but the pastor says I got saved." Still holding my wrists and with a softened voice and demeanor she said "Eric – I want that too." Talk about a day that will live in infamy! I said "OK, well you need to go kneel down over there by the couch in the living room and ask God to come to you like He did for me..." Guess what? God is always on the job! He showed up in our living room AGAIN! What a day! As He gently and deliberately drew us closer to Him and to each other, my wife committed her life and future to the Lord in exactly the same way that I had done only a few days earlier!

He is faithful – He never fails

Here's what I want you to know – God is faithful! He NEVER fails! His word is truth! His ways are the best! And – He wants to share His eternal, risen, powerful, love-filled life with all of us – His most precious creation! Want to talk about good news? This is *The Good News.* This is the Gospel of Jesus Christ!

I'll abbreviate the rest of the story. Three years later we adopted our second child – another precious little girl – tiny, she weighed less than 5 pounds! Six months after that we left California to attend three years of Bible College. Six years later we adopted a son. A year after that we adopted another little girl. Six months after that we adopted another son. And eleven months after that, we adopted another precious little girl! Childless? No, I don't think so!

The runaway freight train of life with the Lord

Oh, I forgot to mention, that in the middle of our run-away freight train of a life, I discovered that I had a son born to a woman I had known in the Air Force before I'd met Deby. Since that time, he and I have reunited. We are still in relationship with each other and have been for over 25 years (that's seven kids for those of you who are counting!). Also, during that time, I was asked to help out at a small church near our Bible College. I then ended up being asked to serve as Senior Pastor upon the sudden and unexpected death of the pastor I had been helping. I continue to serve that same church as pastor to this day.

The Lord has opened doors of foster care, adoption, missions work, international travel and higher education. He has made a way for our children to attend college and has provided a wonderful old turn-of-the-century farmhouse on over twenty-five acres in which to raise the children, to grow in love for each other and to learn to serve in His kingdom. "A second wind indeed."

Are you ready to discover your own SECOND WIND?

"The master key to your success is to keep
moving in the direction of your dream. Things
are going to happen to trip you up. There will
be long dry spells where nothing appears to

be happening. Stay focused on your dream even in the midst of all the disappointments and setbacks and rejections. Keep falling forward. The universe will align itself and respond to your efforts and your energy. There will be times when you may feel "I just can't do this anything more...I'm tired and exhausted." Stay focused on your dream. Dig down deep and know that <u>you will get a second wind</u>. Doors will open that you did not see. Keep the faith, believe in yourself, and hold on to your dream. You have greatness within."[3] (Les Brown)

There's no time like the present

Someone many years ago made an observation that, though it's now become cliché, still holds true. It's a simple but profound statement: "There's no time like the present." Listen! Maybe you should have started a long time ago. Maybe you've been sitting on your dream for many years. Maybe you know that you should have gotten that degree already, or you should have entered the ministry after college, or you wish you had started that business when you were younger. It's probably true that five or ten or thirty

---

[3] Les Brown: World's #1 Motivational Speaker quoted by Dr. Keith Johnson in a personal interview; January 2016

years ago would have been better! Reality check: those days are gone, but today and tomorrow are right in front of you. The sign in front of a little country church recently blared at me, "Two days from now, tomorrow will be yesterday!" Truer motivation for making a decision has never been spoken. Get up and go look at yourself in the mirror right this minute and say, "Today is my day and I'm ready to rock 'n roll – lets' do this!" Today is the day. Now is the time!

Now is the time to "press in"!

I realized something that day I was ready to sell the Harleys. In that moment of darkness and doubt and challenge, and with the help and the prompting of a faithful pastoral friend, I discovered new life. Now IS NOT the time to back down! I discovered that now is not quitting time – now is pressing-in time! It's time to press in to destiny. It's time to press in to purpose. It's time to press in to God and His guidance and His leadership and His power. It's SECOND WIND TIME! It's time to launch those dreams, do that work and to experience the joy of anointed success in the presence and the power of the God who NEVER gives up. A God who, especially, never gives up on you and me! And by the way, I'm pleased to report that Deby and I are still in the race and running stronger than ever! But listen, enough about us, now it's your Second Wind time! Let's just see what God will do!

"I won't give up – I cannot be defeated – I will not quit"
Rev. Kenneth Hagin Jr.

Second Wind Principles

Read:

Ephesians 6:13 The Message – "Be prepared...take all the help you can get...so that when it's all over but the shouting you'll still be on your feet."

Reflect:

The New King James Bible says it more traditionally: "...take up the whole armor of God, that you may be able to withstand in the evil day, and having done all, to stand." Have you reached the end of your "rope"? Have you prayed, read Scripture, begged, pleaded, talked to your friends and cried to your family? Have you done everything you know to do? Then "having done all," it's time to stand! Stand in faith. Stand in confidence. Stand open to personal change. Stand knowing that better days are just around the corner!

<u>Reset:</u>

1. What is one area of your life you want to see changed? (Relationally, Professionally, Spiritually, Personally)

   _____

2. Where can you go (on-line, library, counselor, friend, Scripture, prayer) to discover a few action steps that may help make that change?

   _____

3. What one action/activity can you employ in the next day or two that will take you one step closer to jump-starting the change needed for your new life?

   _____

Chapter 2

OUTWARD GROWTH

Acts 6:1 "The church was multiplying..."

E veryone wants growth! We all want our efforts to pay off. Last spring, we planted a home garden for the first time in years. It was a lot of work (that might be why it's been such a long time since we've had a garden!) We broke the ground, we tilled it, we raked it, we picked out the rocks, we raked it some more, we picked out more rocks. Finally, we got it planted. From the next day and virtually every day after that I went to the fence to look at the garden...I went to look for growth. Within a week or so the first signs of new life began to show and by the time 3 weeks had passed we were full-fledged gardeners – experts in the arena of subsistence living! It was a great summer and we got a lot of vegetables from that little plot of ground. It was so good, in fact, we are looking forward to planting it again for future summers.

One thing that caught us off guard was the speed at which the weeds could grow! It seemed that they could multiply faster than we could pick their vegetable-choking, harvest-threatening little carcasses out of there. While the desired vegetable growth was motivating, the need to continually tend, weed, and cultivate surprised us. My grandmother used to say, after a prolonged time without visiting, "O my Eric, you are growing like a weed". I think I've got the picture now! As fast as the garden grew, the rest of creation, including the weeds, was growing right along with it.

The Book of Acts makes me nervous!

The "garden" is growing. The church is expanding, the Holy Spirit is showing up, and people are coming to the Lord from everywhere. It's every church or business leader's dream – "Exponential Growth"! And in the midst of it all...Weeds! Issues! Challenges! The Book of Acts makes me nervous because when I read the narrative and put myself in the position of the early leaders, I feel like it's all one step from going completely haywire!

"If everything is under control you're going too slow"
(Mario Andretti)

The story began with Jesus and twelve disciples and that seems manageable enough. By the time we get to Acts 1:15

the writer observes that "altogether the number of names (present in an 'upper room' v.13) was about a hundred and twenty" – Okay, one hundred and twenty – a ten-fold increase – but even that is do-able. The Apostle Paul mentioned in 1Corinthians 15:6 that "He (Jesus) was seen by over five hundred brethren at once". Five hundred? That's alright, we're still in the ball-park...we've got some motivated lay ministers and volunteers who are willing to lend a hand, we'll be OK. Acts 2:41 "about three thousand souls were added to them". Whoa! What? Did I read that right? This growth thing is getting a little out of control and besides that, someone took my regular seat during the worship service last Sunday! Acts 2:47 "the Lord added to the church daily". In Acts 4:4 "the number of men came to be about 5000" (we don't know how many women and children were added during that time) and in Acts 5:14 "believers were increasingly added... multitudes of both men and women". We don't even know how many people *that* represents! We already know the recorders of the Book of Acts can count to 120, 500, 3000 and 5000. Now they've reached a point where they've quit counting. They're not even "ball-parking" the attendance – "multitudes". It's as if the writer is saying – "trust me, it's a whole bunch of people!"

A few "small" details...

Here's the point. This all happened within weeks after the Lord had ascended to heaven and shortly after the first post-resurrection church meetings began. In a brief period, less time than many churches require for "membership privileges" to be extended to new attenders, the church had grown from a handful to in excess of ten thousand souls! Overnight success! Yes!

But consider a few "small" details. They have no administration, no buildings, no echelon of command, no experience (this has never been done before), no banks or treasurers or deacons or ushers or, or, or...! Someone once advised me "be careful what you pray for, you just might get it". Was someone praying for numerical growth?

Growing can get messy...

Once while attending a lecture by the founding pastor of a large church of about 6500 members near Seattle Washington, the mega-church pastor began querying the audience, mostly pastors along with church and business leaders. "How many of you would like to have 6500 people?" Just about every hand went up. "How many of you would like to have the money from that many people?" He had just shared how in a recent service; they had received a one-time offering of over a million dollars for their building campaign.

In fact, the pastor had shared that the offering was so large that they had to hire an armored car company to transport it to the bank! Oh Yeah – I think EVERY hand went up as if to say "You can bet I'd like that kind of money". But then he asked the wake-up-and-smell-the-coffee question: "How many of you would like to deal with the problems of 6500 people?" I can't be sure, but I believe NO hands went up on that one!

It's easy to lose sight of the fact that when growth occurs there are both positive and negative collateral effects. "An empty stable stays clean, but no income comes from an empty stable." (Proverbs 14:4 NLT) The "stable" stays clean when there's nothing happening on the farm but an unproductive (i.e. clean) farm has no life, no health and no prosperity. In fact, it's not really a farm at all – it's just a field with some buildings and fences on it. Our lives, our future, our families, our businesses, our churches are intended by God to be much more than an empty (clean) field punctuated with a few out-buildings. Just remember and be ready to embrace the fact that growing, whether it be a church or a business or a household, can get "messy".

> *"Leadership recognizes a problem*
> *before it becomes and emergency"*
> (Arnold Glasow)

"I know a little Greek"

The New Testament was written in Greek[4]. While this is not intended to be an in-depth Greek-to-English word study, some non-English reference resources have been utilized to expand, expound and highlight first-century words, thoughts, customs and principles. A mentor during my early training was Rev. Bob Mumford. Always up for a joke or to poke fun at the way we "do business" as Christians, he once began a sermon by saying "I know a little Greek...he owns a delicatessen down on Thirty-third and Main." It was Bob's way of refusing to distance himself from everyday folks by intimidating them with "secret knowledge" gained from his years of study and experience in the original Biblical languages.

The value of authorial intent

It is my heartfelt desire to include all levels of reader scholarship. At the same time we must not lose sight of the fact that there is often value to be gained from embracing a more complete and detailed Scriptural meaning of Biblical words. This greater depth of understanding is gained by thorough study of the original languages. Without insights into the Bibles' original wording some of the depth of the authorial intent (the authors' intended purpose and message) of

---

[4] Some portions of the New Testament were penned in Aramaic, an ancient and extinct 1st century middle eastern language

a given passage may be overlooked or lost. Please note that a determined effort has been made throughout this work not to complicate or obfuscate Biblical understanding. With that thought in mind, we must at the same time be reminded that any serious student of the Bible should not rely solely upon English translation efforts. Working along those lines, let us explore an exciting reality in the opening sentence of Chapter 6:

"...the number of disciples was *multiplying...*"
(Acts 6:1 italics added).

In this case the Greek word translated to the English word *"multiplying"* has depth not immediately obvious in English. In the Greek language the word "Plethuno" (play-thoo'-no) means to fill or be full. Reference the English word "plethora" meaning "a great quantity" or an overwhelming number. Think of it this way; everyone loves to "be full" or to have a full plate or a full wallet. Most of us love the idea of a full church! Plethuno can mean "fulfill" as in the fulfilling of a vision or a calling or a destiny. Plethuno can reference an "increase, a company, a throng or a multitude"[5]. Growth is happening! Eureka! Success at last! The church is abounding, multiplication is occurring, the place is filling up,

---

[5] Strong's Exhaustive Concordance of the Bible; Strong, Dr. James; Hendrickson Pub 1890; NT #4129

"We're growing, it's so awesome, God is here, Look at all the new people, It's all coming together!"

Growth does not mean absence of challenge...

Jesus said "I have come that they would have life and that more abundantly" (John 10:10). This is it folks! God is good! Life is amazing! It doesn't get any better than this! Dr. Eugene Peterson in The Message Bible brings a gut-level shot of reality to our idyllic ignorance: "The disciples were increasing in numbers by leaps and bounds...and hard feelings developed..." (Acts 6:1). The New Living Translation puts it this way "as the believers rapidly multiplied, *there were rumblings of discontent*". WHAT? You said it's all good! Hard feelings? Challenges? Unhappy people? Somewhere in the course of events, many of us have embraced the idea that growth equals absence of challenge or hardship. If I had to re-entitle this portion of the Bible I think I'd like to call it "NORMAL CHURCH"! Challenge is normal. Hardship happens. Struggles develop in the best of scenarios. We are people. We push. We push forward. Sometimes life pushes back!

One reason we struggle when we face push-back in everyday life is that we have under-estimated the amount of effort and the level of exertion that goes along with success. We often gear-up for failure but have no end-game in mind for those times that we succeed! We come up with alternatives and Plan-B's and possible course corrections or stop-gaps to be employed if things begin to struggle. I don't know if the first church had a plan B or not. Regardless, it would seem to be irrelevant because plan A worked! They trusted God, they prayed, they obeyed, they followed His lead and He brought them into a miraculous and marvelous time of multiplication, the likes of which had never been seen before. Beautiful! But now what?

Everyone braces for failure

Everyone braces for failure but does anyone really consider the complications that can arise from succeeding? Success, like failure, can create an environment of struggle! When we fail, we deal with the failure. We treat it like our enemy and we push ahead. We try new "angles" and fresh action plans, and try to just keep going. When we succeed we face the common human tendency of just getting by, of simply maintaining the status quo. The inclination to take Peter's top-of-the- Mount-of-Transfiguration-approach is tempting – "Let's build three shelters and just hang out here for a while." (Matthew 17:4, paraphrase) But God isn't generally in the "just hang out" business. What happens when holding steady isn't good enough? Success itself is a form of push back! Once we've known a level of success, it can haunt us with the sense that we could do better. Or worse, that we should work to protect our victories from those who might try to adjust, change or improve upon them.

"If you get puffed up you're headed for a blow-out"
(Rev. Ruth Rodriguez)

Success can be almost as wearying as failure

"Stress...is the name given to the normal internal physiological mechanism that adapts us to change...Distress is the negative, destructive aspect of this mechanism...Eustress is the positive, constructive aspect of the adaptation response... Eustress energizes us. It is what football players call "psyching up" before a game. Eustress makes us especially creative before a deadline...it is what wakes a sleeping mother when she hears an infant stirring in the next room...she arises alert and ready to go..."[6]

Interestingly, positive stress still produces "stressors" (changes that trigger a response). The result – success can be almost as wearying as failure!

"Good enough" is not good enough!

An alternate and opposite response to success can be placation. That's when we find ourselves saying "it's good enough". It's not necessarily out of a laid back or lazy attitude, but out of the exhaustion produced by the effort we've expended in pursuit of the journey to this point. Once we

---

[6] Swenson, Richard A. M.D.; "Margin..."; Navpress 1992; p. 59

have attained a measure of success, we have a fallback position that we know we can maintain. I've had people say to me "why are you always changing things" or "if it works don't fix it". Those are fallback or maintenance attitudes. We find that we are willing to lock-in to that satisfactory experience, or method. It is common to start defining success by what has been seen so far. The people of the Book of Acts had never seen or imagined most of what they began to experience. They were not limited by "common sense", or science, or "rules of probability". The Holy Spirit seemed intent upon establishing new days with new ways. The people were led to embrace their success with hearts and minds open to God's direction and an ever-increasing dependence upon God's moment by moment intervention, protection and provision.

A favorite devotional of mine lambasts the "fallback" or "good-enough" approach to living our lives. In an anthology of sermons by early Twentieth-century healing evangelist Smith Wigglesworth he comments "God has no place for a person who is stationary".[7] His contention is that there is no such thing as staying static in God...we are always growing – either closer to or further from God and resultantly, His will, His call, His ways, His care, His concern, His power and His favor. In other words, "Good enough" is not good enough!

Acts chapter 6 is specifically about the growth of the church, but the application of the principles and experiences

---

gleaned from that pursuit, can be utilized to grow in other contexts as well. Insights from the first-century church can be adapted to fit our lives today. We can learn to grow ourselves, to grow the people around us (spouse, children, employees, co-workers, neighbors, fellow Christians), to grow a business, to grow a support group or to grow a ministry.

Next Level Vision

We live in a world that wonders "what next" or "what now". Many in our culture struggle. Many do not have a true direction; they are not able to "discern the times" (1Chronicles 12:32). They are unknowing of what to do or where to turn. The Apostle Paul compared our current condition with that of an unguided child, tossed by every "wind of doctrine" (every teaching, every hypothesis or conjecture); having no "moral compass" upon which to depend. Many do not know whom or what to trust while navigating the storms of life (Ephesians 4:14 paraphrase).

God's tools

Vision, destiny, hope and the anticipation of a positive outcome are the tools God uses to change our minds, to change our behavior, to change us. His plan to GROW US has taken the "lid" off our potential. We now know that because His hand is NOT too short (Isaiah 50:2, 59:1) and because His ways are higher than our ways (Isaiah 55:9) that nothing is impossible for Him (Luke 1:37). That truth includes raising us to the next level He has in store for our lives.

> *"Quit something that doesn't make a difference*
> *and do something that does"*
> (Dr. John Maxwell)

God is seeking the best possible outcome for our lives

"Where there is no vision (no redemptive revelation of God), the people perish..." (Proverbs 29:18 The Amplified Bible). A "redemptive revelation of God" is the realization that we are never outside of His care or beyond His reach. He will always pull for you. His plan is always to help and to "leverage" new heights and broader expanses into your thinking and your planning. He is moving us toward bigger faith, more courage, stronger confidence, deeper conviction. In short, God is seeking the best possible outcome for our lives!

- Deborah had a vision in Judges, chapters four and five, of Israel conquering her enemies – she acted upon it and led her nation to victory
- Nehemiah had a vision for rebuilding the broken down wall and the decimated city of Jerusalem, he sought God for a plan and against all odds he pulled it off in less than two months! (Nehemiah 4:1-6:16)

- Elisha was surrounded by enemies on all sides, he had an encounter with the Lord in which he realized "many more are those who are for us than those who are against us" (2Kings 6:16).
- Ruth had a vision to serve her mother-in-law and make "your God – my God" (Ruth 1:16-17). She went down in history as one of the most noble people who have ever lived and a great-great-great (times twenty-five "greats") – grandmother of Jesus
  o What if you knew that what you do, say, believe, act upon today has an impact on a person two generations from now – or ten generations or twenty-five generations?
- Peter had a vision of a sheet let down from heaven – during the experience he received correction from God that he was not to look down upon anyone, their heritage, background, culture or customs from that time forward – when he embraced it and acted upon it the vision served to transform evangelism for all eternity (Acts 10:9ff / 11:4ff).

Stop and ask yourself:

- "Am I growing"? "In what ways"? "How fast"?
- "How have I grown recently"? "Am I satisfied with my progress"?

- "What is my vision, my hope and my expectation for future direction and growth and progress"?

HOW TO CULTIVATE PERSONAL GROWTH–THREE STEPS:

Step 1 – Feed the Growth –

Dr. Mike Brown makes the point that: "Whatever you honor draws closer, whatever you dishonor moves further away"[8] Similarly one could then conclude that, "What we feed grows and what we starve dies."

- In the spring Deby, my wife, likes to plant annuals – One year we waited too long and all the flowers at the store looked shriveled and anemic; they looked sorrier than a Charlie Brown Christmas tree in my opinion. But she wanted 'em so we brought them home!
- To my surprise, with some water, some Miracle Gro and a little TLC, that year we had the best flowers ever! Why? Because what we feed will grow!
- Our lives, our church, our families, our jobs or schools or teams are like that: Whatever we feed with prayer and love and care and time – grows.

---

[8] Brown, Dr. Mike; "The Lost Diamond of Honor"; Strong in the Lord Ministries; 2005; p. 25

Conversely, if we feed doubt and fear and worry and negativism – those things will grow too!

When we spend time in worship and the Word of God and Fellowship with each other – We grow AND the people around us grow!

Step 2- Practice the Growth —

Look for opportunities to serve

- "Your people shall be volunteers in the day of Your power..." (Psalms 110:3)
- "Your people will offer themselves willingly..." (Psalms 110:3 Amplified Bible)

"God loves a cheerful giver" (2Corinthians 9:7) God is not looking for stuff, He is looking for people – Hearts and lives that will give and love and serve Him.

Step 3- Anticipate the Growth / Expect it / Look for it / Manage it –

- Jesus gave a whole teaching about a servant who buried his talent (his GROWTH POTENTIAL) and how displeased the master was with his laid back wimpy approach (Matthew 25:28ff)
  - o The servant failed to expect good things and promise and reward – consequently he completely missed what God wanted to do in his life

- Hebrews 11:6 ...without faith it is impossible to please Him, for <u>he who comes to God must believe that He is, and that He is a rewarder of those who diligently seek Him</u>.
  - o His nature is love and His default mode is blessing!
  - o His prerequisite is simple...BELIEVE!
- Gods promise, God's Will, God's Plan for our lives is always Growth – Personal, Corporate, Physical, Spiritual, Relational – All aspects of our lives should be *"focused forward"* looking for the good stuff in Him and from Him!
- Our High School Track Coach yells from the sideline: "Don't look back – The race is in front of you!!"

You are on God's team and you can expect great things from Him – Your future is in front of you. Keep looking forward–Anticipate Growth!!

Second Wind Principles

Read:

When John the Baptist was thrown into prison he began to wonder if he had "jumped the gun" with his endorsement of Jesus – he was getting close to running on empty and needed a Second Wind! Listen to the reply Jesus sent back to John:

Jesus...said to them, "Go and tell John the things you have seen and heard: that <u>the blind see</u>, <u>the lame walk</u>, <u>the lepers are cleansed</u>, <u>the deaf hear</u>, <u>the dead are raised</u>, <u>the poor have the gospel preached</u> to them. And blessed is he who is not offended ("tripped up"–Strong's #4624 NT) because of Me." (Luke 7:22-23)

Relate:

We can get "tripped up" when we get blind-sided by challenges in our daily lives. Where is God? Does He care? Is He at work? Has He forgotten me? List a few areas of life in which you would like to see an increase of God's influence

_____

React:

1. What evidence can you see of God's work in the world around you?_____
2. When have you experienced a "Second Wind" in life?

_____

3. What areas can use a "Second Wind" right now?

_____

Chapter 3

INNER CONFLICT

Acts 6:1 "There arose a complaint…"

S piritual Health does not necessarily mean complete peace and ease! Just when everyone thought the sky was the limit and things couldn't get any better, a challenge arises in the ranks. Struggle and complaint are not always a bad thing as long as someone in the group can grasp the redemptive value offered by constructive criticism. When the parties involved can avoid the quagmire of destructive back-biting and negativism, an even greater advancement can often be realized.

"Anyone can hold the helm when the sea is calm"
(Publius Syrus – Circa 85-43 BC)

Building instead of bulldozing

As a pastor I have conducted many wedding ceremonies. Prior to the couple's embarkation upon the journey of marriage I request a few appointments together to share some thoughts about their lives and the future in the context of covenant marriage. One question I always ask during these sessions is: "What is it like when you guys argue?" Anyone who has been married longer than a few months knows what I'm talking about! Just when one spouse thinks things can't get any better, from their partner there will "arise a complaint"! An issue! A problem!

A challenge! While there is no right or wrong answer to my argument question, I expect to hear that at least one of them raises their voice. Or one gets quiet and withdrawn. Or one will walk out or say they "need some space". I'm hoping to get the chance to give some constructive advice on how to turn an argument into a productive growth experience that will serve to build rather than bulldoze the relationship.

Argument can be a great opportunity

Sometimes a couple, when asked regarding their habits during an argument, will insist that they don't argue or "we never fight" – to which my first thought is "Well then, let's discontinue this session until AFTER you've had a fight and take it back up at that time!" Someone will say, "Don't you think you're being a little cynical?" Perhaps, but what I know from pastoring, from my own family and from life in general is this – People disagree with one another! Every marriage (or business or church or workplace) is going to have times of disagreement. The Lord God invited Isaiah "Come, let us *argue* this out" (Isaiah 1:18 NLT) several versions say something to the effect of "let us *reason* together". The Lord in His infinite wisdom extends a redemptive invitation: "Let us examine our various perspectives and see what we can learn and how we can improve our outcome."

An argument or disagreement can be a great opportunity for a new perspective. A conflict, especially one motivated by constructive criticism, can open our eyes to alternative solutions. Just as a difference of opinion in marriage can lead to a more solid, inclusive and satisfying long-term relationship; a challenge to tradition or "how we've always done it" or the surfacing of some new unexpected struggle in church or business can be just the impetus we need to effect fresh possibilities for prolonged growth.

Expansion causes struggle

In the Acts 6 narrative, "there arose a complaint"! Of course there are problems! There is always tension in growth! Expansion causes struggle – "growing pains" result from reconfiguring and stretching and accommodating. New needs, unforeseen expectations, past hurts or bad experiences – all factor together to produce the unexpected consequence of unsettled or dissatisfied participants. How many stories have we heard of a church installing new carpet or paint only to find that someone is irate over the change from what it "used to be"? New pastors about to assume their first role as senior leader are advised "Whatever you do, don't start making changes too soon". Why is that? It's because Sister So-and-So or Brother What's-his-Name will be upset because "they don't like change".

The foyer looked good

I once consulted at a small country church that was in chaos because the former pastor had insisted upon painting the entry foyer of the church building. I emphasize the word "former" as he was no longer there for two reasons. First was the painting of the entry. Secondly he had failed to make sure he mowed the lawn on Saturdays! I was more than a little perplexed as upon entering the church, the first thing that caught my eye was how good the foyer looked! It was beautiful, especially when compared to the rest of the building. It was an older church, the carpets were a bit thread-bare, the paint was chipped, the windows needed cleaning, it had that "old church smell" – I think you get the picture. The entry, by contrast, was fantastic! It was bright and fresh and smelled nice, the windows were clean. The former pastor had installed new French doors with beveled glass – it was a great first impression. Unfortunately, it was the only room that had that look and feel – and sadly the board had "sent him packing" before he could affect the rest of the makeover.

Mow the lawn on Saturday or get fired on Monday!

So I met with this church board and listened as they enumerated the failures of the previous pastor citing his remodeling and painting of the entry and his failure to make sure he mowed the lawn on Saturdays. Their second criticism of the pastor really stumped me and I asked about it. I was instructed in no uncertain terms that Saturday mowing was necessary to assure that the church looked its best on Sunday mornings. For the record, I agree that a freshly mowed lawn makes a place look sharp. The part I couldn't understand was why it would be the pastor's job to do the mowing!

As it turned out, many (perhaps many, many) years ago the church had had an old-time country pastor who had been raised on a farm and loved the smell of freshly cut hay. The closest he could get to the reproduction of that sweet aroma was the essence arising from a newly manicured lawn. Thus, he made it clear to the board (many of whom were still at the church long after that pastor had moved on) that he would like part of his summer duties to include mowing the lawn. He stipulated that the church should provide the tractor or mower and that his preference was to mow on Saturday so the place would look great on Sunday morning.

Challenge comes as a by-product of success

It all made sense once I'd heard the entire story. What the board didn't realize is that things change. Growth comes. Different people have different preferences and priorities. The paint that looked great in 1987 looks a little faded, chipped and worn in 2017. The man who loved mowing the lawn and made it a priority in his ministry those many years ago is not the same man who will assume the pulpit this weekend to deliver what he feels the Lord has laid upon his heart for this gathering of His flock. A new day requires a new approach! The complaint arose out of a need to adapt the methods and ministry to the new day and the new growth that God had granted. You could say that the challenge came as a by-product of their success!

What if the disciples or the Hellenistic widows in the Acts story had said "That's it, I'm done, there's no way I'm going to this church anymore?" Not only would the growing church have been hindered, but had they given up they would have cut themselves off from being part of one of the greatest Kingdom success stories ever seen on planet Earth! I wonder how many pastors or church members or business owners or employees, because of some in-house challenge or struggle or "complaint", quit just as things are beginning to succeed and growth is really starting to occur?

From zero to hero to zero

It is a true statement that people who never try never fail. But listen to this caveat: those who never try will never fail – AND they will never *really* succeed either! There is always tension with growth. If you don't believe it, decide today that you will become a weight lifter. Now go to the gym and spend a couple of hours trying to bench press as much weight as you can. Go ahead, and start out with two or three hundred pounds on the bar! You'll sweat and huff and puff for a while then go back to the office and all will seem fine... UNTIL tomorrow morning when you try to get out of bed! At that moment every muscle in your body will awaken and with one voice they will cry out "you are an idiot" while they commence aching, throbbing and resisting your every move. What happened? You tried to "grow" without adapting yourself to the process required. Muscle growth is an excellent goal with tons of available information on how to do it carefully and correctly. In our example we should have begun with manageable weight and limited repetitions, increasing both over time until we got to the desired level of fitness. Instead of going from "zero to hero" we went from "zero to hero to zero" – the pain in our body will testify to that truth!

All great moves of God produce conflict

What? All great moves of God produce human conflict, confusion and competition? "Well that can't be right!" Can it? "If it's God it's good!" Some have mistakenly confused walking in the will of God with guaranteed ease of outcome. Just take a look at history:

- Moses faces the Red Sea in its full fury – the water did not part until Moses acted by raising his staff and ordering the people forward (Exodus 14:15-16) How would you like to have been at the head of *that* line?

- Joshua's plan for the breaching Jericho consists of walking around in armor and blowing horns culminating with a great shout (Joshua 6:3-7)! "OK that's sure to work! Not!"

- John the Baptist is thrown in jail and begins to have second thoughts about Jesus—"Is He the One or should we expect another?" A logical question considering the fact that John has put his whole life on the line for this message and is now facing execution. Jesus answers "tell John what you've seen and heard... the blind see, the lame walk, the lepers are cleansed, the deaf hear, the dead are raised, the poor have the gospel preached to them..." (Luke 7:22) – "It's OK John, we're in this together..."

I draw courage from these stories because I can see myself facing my own struggles and having the same types of doubts and questions.

God is not limited...and neither are we!

I enjoy reading the early prophets. Isaiah says "Woe is me, I am undone!" (Isaiah 6:5). My interpretation of that passage is more like "Oh brother, I'm in trouble now!" At one-point God explains to Isaiah why the prophet is having difficulty in his attempts to anticipate or accept the words and actions of the Lord he is determined to serve. Difficulties are virtually certain because:

"...My thoughts are not your thoughts, Nor are your ways My ways," says the LORD. "For as the heavens are higher than the earth, So are My ways higher than your ways, And My thoughts than your thoughts." (Isaiah 55:8-9)

There is an "understanding gap" between God's ways and our ways. We struggle with the deflection between His thoughts and His resources and our ability to understand Him. His refusal to be defined within the scope of our limited comprehension is a constant source of challenge and struggle for us. His vision sees beyond our purview. His methods never lack provision. He doesn't lie awake wondering how to make a monthly payment or how to grow a certain segment of the business or the ministry. He simply explains "I'm not limited in my abilities and neither are you IF you will only believe and follow"!

Old problems or new solutions...the choice is ours

Often, in our world, old problems seem more comfortable than new solutions. Sometimes it seems easier to just stay where we are than to deal with the challenges created by the implementation of new ideas and methods. Even if what I'm doing today has its problems and limitations, it is familiar and I know how to work with it or around it. As soon as we try to go beyond where we've been – expand the business, hire some new people, add a new department, reconfigure a ministry, re-position a staff member – then comes the "complaint". Reluctance to change begins to show itself. Sometimes the resistance is so great that the leader will conclude that the growth just isn't worth the hassle required to make the change happen. Thus begins the cycle of decline for the organization. As long as our group is driven by fear of failure or reluctance to face the challenge or worry that the complaint will be the end of us, then we will be inclined to either deliberately ignore or just plain miss altogether the opportunities for growth as they present themselves.

"Old problems are more comfortable than new solutions"
(Author Unknown)

We are all tempted to procrastinate

We may not like the problems but at least we've grown used to them. We know how to placate or delay them and continue on our way until another season of time. A friend of mine says "Never do today what you can put off until tomorrow!" I think he actually has that backwards – the saying is "Never put off until tomorrow what you can do today." The temptation to procrastinate in the difficult or the uncomfortable is a challenge we all face on a regular basis.

A church elder once commented – "I don't see why we have to keep growing all the time!" Another member of that same group commented "All I ever hear is the need to change, I like my little church just the way it is." We all have comfort levels. We get used to the way we've done it in the past. Early in my ministry career an older churchman challenged my youth – "I have twelve years of experience in this ministry" – he said! I looked at him and asked "Brother, do you have twelve years of experience, or do you have one year of experience twelve times?" I grant you, that was a little "in your face" and could probably have been said better, but the point is well-taken that growth, by nature, will require change. How many people do you know who face one change, struggle or problem after another yet seemingly never grow from any of it?

Don't settle for what has always been done

Our churches are full of people who have settled-in to the way things have "always been done" but they fail to realize that the system, the music, the décor they hold so near and dear was at one time the product of the changes effected by an earlier generation. For example, throughout the centuries secular music has been borrowed and "re-branded" to be appropriate for congregational use. Famous hymn writers such as Martin Luther, John and Charles Wesley, Fannie Crosby, Charles Spurgeon and William Booth (founder of the Salvation Army) have been either accused or credited (depending upon one's viewpoint) with attempting to bring the secular into the sacred. [9]

Failure to recognize and embrace the change and the advancement occurring in the world around us has resulted in the widely held perception that religion in general and church in particular are irrelevant to most people and to most of life's challenges. The sad result of that assumption is that many who might receive help and encouragement are left feeling that they have nowhere to turn and no one to care while opportunity is just a prayer or a phone call or a worship service away.

---

[9] Manfred F. Bukofzer, 'Popular and Secular Music in England', The New Oxford History of Music 3: Ars Nova and the Renaissance, 1300-1540, ed. Anselm Hughes and Gerald Abraham (London: Oxford University Press, 1960), p. 108.

"Many of life's failures are people who did not realize how close they were to success when they gave up!"
(Thomas Edison)[10]

Spiritual "porkers"...

Equally distressing are those who attend the church and claim the Name of the Lord yet live life as if they are on their own. They call their own shots. They make their own rules. They are the folks who show up every week but bring nothing but a bad attitude and a critical spirit. They are quick to judge and they continually decry the accusation that they aren't being "fed".

Rev. John Maxwell, in a sermon many years ago, referred to them as "Spiritual Porkers" – people who belly-up to the feed trough (the church) once a week to sample the "food" then get fatter by the month never really growing or going anywhere in the things of God. In spite of their self-imposed prison of mediocrity and go-nowhere-do-nothing lifestyle, they are always ready to complain, withhold their giving and "abandon ship" whenever their behavior is challenged. We need to ask ourselves if we are becoming "spiritually flabby" or are we being "toned" and developed by the Word of God and by His Holy Spirit?

---

[10] Cordeiro, Wayne; "Leading on Empty"; Bethany House, 2009; p.202

Healthy things grow

We can't stay where we are and end up where we want to be! Is dormancy our goal? Is it even an option in God? There is a reality in nature – healthy things are growing things. They are changing. They are morphing. They are vital and relevant and alive. They are active and adaptive and expressive. Sure there are complaints! Everyone in the group, organization, church or company, is feeling the pressure of change drawing them into continual growth and refinement. At various times everyone will feel like they need a break. Go ahead, take a time of refreshing. But then, emulate the attitude of the United States Marine Corps – "Adapt and overcome". Every obstacle, every challenge, every complaint has the potential to teach us or strengthen us or alert us. Circumstances, even the difficult ones, help to grow us. All things work together and become part of the journey that is taking us from where we are to where our God-given calling has destined us to be (Romans 8:28).

"Too many people are living below their privileges"
(Rev. Joel Osteen)

I think the disciples were blind-sided by the complaint that arose Acts 6. I don't think they had in mind to ignore anyone or to fail to connect with any individual or group. They surely didn't intend to eliminate any needy person from the "daily distribution". They took advantage of the opportunities that presented themselves. They preached, laid on hands for healing, counseled, prayed and studied. They were trying to grasp this new dimension of life and spiritual power that had been bequeathed to them at the ascension of Jesus Christ (Mark 16:15-18). In the process of the turnover in leadership and in the manifestation of the power and the growth of the "organization", they found the unexpected collateral outcome of expansion – they discovered the need to reconfigure the way the leadership team was functioning.

The implementation of new leadership styles and methods that adapt to the size and needs of the organization, will bring new insights into the dynamics of change and growth and how to employ them for personal, organizational and Kingdom expansion

Second Wind Principles

Read:

The thief does not come except to steal, and to kill, and to destroy. I have come that they may have life, and that they may have it more abundantly. (John 10:10)

Reflect:

When Jesus says the thief (the devil) "does not come except" – He is saying "your enemy will only come" when he is on a destructive path for you, your life, your family, your church, your nation... Our enemy has but one function – to make life miserable for people! BUT Jesus has come to bring life, good life, great life, abundant life!

- Check out Dr. Jack Hayford's definition of abundance: "Superabundance, excessive, overflowing, surplus, over and above, more than enough, profuse, extraordinary, above the ordinary, more than sufficient"![11]
- Now *THAT'S* a Second Wind!

Reset:

1. Are there any areas "under attack" in your life?

   _____

2. From this passage and Dr. Hayford's definition, what has God promised as His plan for these and other aspects of life? _____

3. What is one step you can take right now to realign your thinking, speaking, believing to accommodate God's good plan? _____

---

[11] Hayford, Dr. Jack; Spirit Filled Life Bible NKJV: Word Wealth Study Note, John 10:10; pg. 1593

Chapter 4

OPENNESS TO CHANGE

Acts 6:2 "...the twelve summoned..."

The French philosopher Voltaire (1694-1778) has been credited with observing that "Good is the enemy of Great". It's ironic that an observation made by an avowed atheist would be so important to modern day Christian leaders. The inherit challenge we face is born out of the fact that solutions to problems are not usually easy to come by. Once a problem is solved, even if it is a stop-gap measure and not a long-term fix, we have the tendency to settle for that repair and even become reluctant to modify it or enhance it as time goes on. It is surprisingly easy to find ourselves in the position of defending "good" as we avoid the work involved in the pursuit of "great". How often have we heard the tongue-in-cheek expression – "If it works, don't fix it"? That is how tradition is born! If it was good enough for Grand-pa, then it's good enough for us (and our kids and grand-kids and their kids...) and we find ourselves facing a 100-year-old less-than-satisfactory solution to some historic situation. The problem itself may not even still exist but we hold to the old ways because "that's how we've always done it!"

Small church, small world

Often, especially in the world of the smaller church, the "solution" to a former issue has become the source of a current problem. To make things even more challenging, there is a reluctance to change. Real struggle often develops as one attempts to adapt past methods in order to address current demands. New issues often require fresh objectivity and new methods to bring us into a more contemporary and relevant alignment with today's needs and concerns. Yesterday's help can become today's hindrance! Good really can get in the way of great!

One may wonder, "Why is the reluctance-to-change issue exacerbated in the smaller church?" It is my assessment that the reason a small church is unusually "set in their ways" lies in the regularity with which we find the smaller church in rural and less populated areas of the country.[12]

---

[12] When I say "smaller" I'm thinking of churches of under 100 or so members and in communities with limited recruitment potential. In general, these gatherings will not be cosmopolitan (varied and open to outside influence) in their makeup.

I live in a very small town. In fact, some have said that we "have more cows than people in our town." To say that we are not demographically diverse would be a huge understatement. The joke in our community is that you can live here twenty years and still be an outsider. That's because everybody *from* here knows everybody *from* here! Essentially, if you weren't born here, your neighbors will always consider you something of a foreigner. When someone asks for directions, for instance, someone will jokingly say "Yer not from around here are ya?" The inference is that if you were from here you'd already know the answer to your question.

What is your standard of measurement?

So what's the problem in the smaller environment? The Apostle Paul warned that "...they (who) measure themselves by themselves and compare themselves with themselves... are not wise" (2 Corinthians 10:12 NIV parentheses added). The context of this passage is an interaction Paul is having with a group who have declared themselves to be apostles. That in itself doesn't seem to be as much of a concern to him as the fact that these "self-appointed apostles" seem to be something of a "good ole' boy society." Apparently they are constantly comparing themselves with each other. It appears that they measure their value, their authority, their anointing and their ministerial status by how they stack up against one another. In an environment with a narrow scope and virtually no outside influence, our potential for cutting-edge solutions to issues is limited to what we already know and to whatever people and resources we currently have on hand.

How much do you know?

Former Secretary of defense Donald Rumsfeld is credited with saying "You only know what you know"[13]. That concept is at the core of the issue the apostle is describing here. If our only frame of reference is what we already know, whenever something new comes along the only interpretation we can offer is based upon our past experiences and not on our current circumstances. It stands to reason that we will interpret current events or proposals through the lens of prior knowledge. The smaller the church (or community or family or business), the narrower the scope of potential resources available to bring to bear upon the concerns we will face.

When we find ourselves in an environment of limited scope and depth, the incumbency is upon each of us to reach out beyond our current limitations so that we may come to a fuller understanding and a better, more carefully considered future outcome for our situation. Our limitations may

---

[13] From a Press Conference at NATO Headquarters, Brussels, Belgium, June 6, 2002 "The message is that there are no "knowns." There are things we know that we know. There are known unknowns. That is to say there are things that we now know we don't know. But there are also unknown unknowns. <u>There are things we do not know we don't know.</u>

be financial, experiential, administrative, relational, educational or spiritual (to name a few). Regardless of the parameters and the conditions that resulted in their development, we, as leaders, are responsible before God and before the people we serve, to go beyond those limitations in order to assure the best possible outcome to our current challenges and to effect the best enablement of future growth.

Their complaint was valid

The Disciples in the Acts 6 narrative, whether incidentally or deliberately, discerned that they were facing an important and potentially divisive issue. They realized the "complaint" was valid and determined to examine and resolve the concern. They called in the "cavalry". They invited advice and help to remedy the challenge! They are faced with a classic case of–that which worked yesterday is not "cutting it" today. So Peter responded to the stated need – he and the other leaders validated the issue–"the problem really does exist". They didn't say "O come on, not the Hellenists again! These people are always belly-aching about something!" Instead they called upon the insights of others whom they trusted to help them discover what was wrong with their methods and to assist them in deciding what could be done to remedy the situation. It takes courage to be in a leadership role and admit that we don't have all the answers all the time! These men saw that the validity of this concern was more important than their personal pride or the appearance that they had it all together or that they had it all figured out. The leaders were willing to hear and to respond to the complaint.

Validation is powerful

There are very few more valuable skills available to the leader than the "art" of validating the feelings, needs, observations and concerns of others. In the early years of ministry when Deby and I were youth workers, one of the top complaints of teen agers was "No one ever listens to me". Concerns that the young people considered to be valid were regularly dismissed or glossed over by the adults around them. One of the teens once asked me "Are we invisible?" What was he asking? "Does anyone really hear what we are saying?" The deeper question and the concern not clearly articulated though definitely inferred was "Do we matter at all to the adults around us?" Everyone wants to know that their thoughts, insights, cares and needs matter to the people around them. They especially want to know that those whom they trust as leaders and authority figures in their lives are aware of and take seriously those same needs and concerns.

Women don't want to be fixed!

Speaking in general terms and along those same lines, when it comes to relationships, men when relating to women tend to adopt the role of "fixers". When a woman makes mention of an area of interaction that she thinks needs discussion and attention, the men have a tendency to either roll their eyes – as if dismissively saying "O brother, the Hellenistic widows again". Or they assume a pontificating role as divine benefactor, the "knight in shining armor" here to "rescue you" and make all your problems disappear. Over the years I've had interactions with dozens of women who say things to the effect of "I don't want him to fix me – I want him to *listen* to me". She is essentially saying just what those teens had said – "No one is listening to me – No one is taking me seriously – My feelings and observations matter".

A powerful reflective listening skill taught in counseling classes is something called "validation." Simply put, validation is the affirmation that the thoughts, feelings, ideas and concerns presented by a person or group are valid. The points raised are justifiable and understandable. When something is valid it is reasonable and recognizable as a logical next step or perhaps the conclusion of a process. When we validate someone's opinion or observation we are not necessarily agreeing with them. That one fact takes a lot of the tension out of the exchange with the person. I don't have to share the same viewpoint as another person to recognize and vocalize that their insights are valid and that their feelings and opinions matter.

Flaming Cornflakes

How does validation work? Think of this scenario: Mom has been at home with the young children all day. The kids have done what kids do – make a mess, argue with each other, produce a bunch of dishes to wash and a pile of clothing that needs laundering – you know the drill. The husband, let's call him Dipstick Dad, comes home. Mom, relieved to see another adult on the property, begins to unpack the days' exploits and foibles. She expresses that she has been on her feet literally for hours and she just needs to sit down for a few minutes. Dad is now facing a dilemma. Will he comfort his wife and save the day? Or will he botch the opportunity to be a blessing? He can say something typically "Dad-ly" like "You think you've had it rough, it's a jungle out there, I've been bust'in my tail all day". He may or may not get dinner that night. Or any meal at all for a couple of days! I once heard of a man, who after having said something uber-stupid, asked his wife for a hot breakfast the next morning. Without batting an eye or missing a beat she sweetly but in no uncertain terms replied – "If you want a hot breakfast, why don't you light your corn flakes on fire?" Probably NOT one of their better days together.

A more satisfying outcome

How could our dad in question have handled things more positively and have experienced a more satisfying outcome for everyone? He could (should) have validated his wife's recounting of her day at home. How about this idea: Wife relays the challenges, struggles, exhaustion of the day complete with a retelling of the messes and subsequent clean-up required. The New Awesome Dad (having read this book) tenderly takes her hand and says "Wow that's an amazing amount of stuff – you must be totally wiped out – why don't you go ahead and sit down for a bit while I go outside and play with the kids, then, when I come in I'll order us a pizza for tonight." Awesome Dad has just hit a home run in his wife's opinion. This is a guy who WILL NOT have to light his corn flakes on fire tomorrow morning!

What did Awesome Dad do that Dipstick Dad did not do? He validated his wife's feelings and her observations of the day. He empathized with her exhaustion and honored the level of work required to live her life. It's not a contest to see who worked the hardest or did the most or invested the most time. Empathy (validation) is simply the recognition that someone has the right to their feelings and observations. It takes no effort at all and it is no threat to us when we validate the feelings, issues or problems of another person. We are never demeaned or diminished when we recognize and exalt the efforts of the people around us. To the contrary, those around us will most likely think MORE of us for caring about the plight of their lives.

This oversight deserves our attention

The first thing the disciples did when they realized that people were being overlooked was that they called together a group of others to examine and try to solve the problem. They validated the concerns and the complaint of the Hellenistic widows. By calling the team together to work on the problem they sent a message to these women that said – "You're right, we blew it, this is an oversight on our part that deserves our full and undivided attention".

At least eight times in the Gospels Jesus says something to the effect of "he who has ears to hear, let him hear" (Matthew 11:15; 13:9 and others). Have you ever tried to share a concern or an observation with someone "without ears to hear", a person who will not listen? As leaders we are in the unique position to not only hear about problems and issues, but we are often equipped with the resources and the abilities to do something about them. What an awesome role of encouragement and forward movement we can inhabit if we are so inclined.

Whenever someone brings a problem to me the first and (I believe) most important thing I can do as a leader is to validate the person and their observation. Admittedly, there are a few people who seemingly exist just to find problems and complain about them. We call those folks "EGRs" or Extra Grace Required people. Just keep in mind not to quickly relegate someone to the "challenging person" category because most people are NOT EGRs! The vast majority of people want to be a part, they want to excel, they want your company or your family or your ministry to be excellent and they are willing to go out on a limb and risk upsetting you or bringing negative attention to themselves in order to apprise you of a situation that they have concluded is worthy of their leaders' attention.

Ask three questions of every problem

When someone brings one of these concerns to my attention I always tell them that I want to discuss three things in response to their observation. For those who are on our staff this three-fold interaction is a prerequisite for bringing the problem to me in the first place. When someone brings a problem I ask:

- What is the problem as you see it? (I prefer the abbreviated version).
- What are at least three options that you think may address the issue?
- What do YOU think should be done about this concern?

This three-pronged approach does a number of things for us:

- It validates the person by recognizing the value of their concern
- It causes them to think about the issue and present it clearly and succinctly
- It brings an immediate potential for collaboration between them and the leaders by seeking their input for proposed solution(s)
- It suggests a possible fix for the problem (a basic rule of leadership is solving problems at the lowest possible level – it's likely that the people closest to the problem will have very good insights as to how to fix it – all they need is our approval and permission)
- Finally, this feedback session endorses the person, considers their ideas and motivates them to be more deeply invested and involved in the forward-movement of the group.

Just look at all the "wins" racked up in this one exchange. The entire discussion will probably take less than 30 minutes of the leaders' time while simultaneously touching on at least 5 positive, value-added aspects of the relationship between the leader and the person with whom they are interacting.

"Change is inevitable – Growth is optional"

Author, coach and public speaker Dr. John Maxwell emphasizes the reality that growth is a personal choice by declaring "Change is inevitable, Growth is optional".[14] What an eye-opening statement!

Someone once told me – "As long as you are alive you must work at changing your environment because when you die your environment is going to work at changing you!" I grant you this is not the most pleasant context in which to imagine our end of life scenario, but the message is an important one. We can spend our lives enduring change. We can resist the advancements of the world around us. We can struggle and advocate to keep things the same as they've always been. Some will just continually remind everyone of the "good old days" lamenting the past and "how good it used to be." Meanwhile, the current days are slipping by one after another. Change is happening all around us but growth is not! We can blow off the thoughts, opinions and preferences of the younger generation, but we can't stop the fact that they will ultimately assume the responsibilities of leadership in every possible area of life on this planet. Change is inevitable – it is coming and it is going to happen – it *is happening*! We can choose to embrace that fact and become part of the discussion and part of the process, or we can

---

[14] 50 Inspirational John C. Maxwell Quotes, Blogpost of Joel Brown, CEO of "Addicted2Success.com" Sept 2015

struggle and chafe and push back. At the end of the day (or at the end of our strength) those changes, those ideas, those people will outlast us. The choice whether to grow or not belongs to each one of us. Always remember this, regardless of our decision, the changes are coming!

A new paradigm

The leaders and the followers in Acts 6 effected change that produced growth! They chose to enter a new paradigm of service-based ministry and achieved tremendous results with their first attempt. New leaders were discovered and appointed, the problem of people being overlooked was addressed and solved. The integrity of the leadership and their desire to learn and grow was demonstrated, a clear path for complaint and resolution was marked out. All of this value was added because they took the time to evaluate the concern and approach it as if it had merit. They believed that a positive outcome could improve their overall "administrative operation" and they were willing to pursue that course to a productive end.

The lesson here is pretty straight-forward. As leaders and especially as caregivers we must be constantly reviewing, evaluating and reconfiguring our systems, procedures, training, personnel and assignments. The Apostle Paul wasn't on the scene in Acts 6 but later, in Romans 12:2 he gives strong advice: "...do not be conformed to this world (and the world's way of doing things) but be transformed ("changed") by the renewing of your mind..." (Parentheses added)

The bigger picture here for the Christian is an admonition by example to change from our everyday methods of dealing with issues to a more God-oriented and "Kingdom-minded" approach to daily life. An immediate application of Romans 12 in this case suggests that once we open our minds to the changes that God is bringing, then we are positioned to arrive at solutions and methods of operation that formerly were unknown to us. Our functionality as people in general and leaders in particular will be flooded with new levels of grace, patience, power and possibility each in greater measure than that which we have previously known.

What is belief?

The Apostle Paul, in his final discourse with his spiritual son, Timothy exhorts "I am not ashamed for <u>I know whom I have believed</u> and I am persuaded (convinced) that He is able to keep what I have committed to Him until that day..." (2Timothy 1:12, Parenthesis added).

> "What is belief? To believe is to know Him in whom I believe—not a vague knowledge of the word "Jesus"—but belief in His nature, His vision, His power, His availability to our lives. His greatness is in you and is greater than he

who is in the world (1John 4:4) ...<u>everything</u> <u>not like our God must go</u> —- <u>seek to release</u> <u>the various parts of your life to His power and</u> <u>love until every part is submitted and trans-</u> <u>formation is complete."</u> [15]

Belief takes us beyond conformity with the world around us. As we submit every part of our thinking, speaking and relating to our "Jesus belief system." The One in whom we believe begins to present Himself to others *through* us! Our attitudes change, our assumptions change, our abilities are enhanced and magnified; our assessments of people and situations become more accurate, our actions are viable and effective.

People vs. Programs

A bumper sticker I once read said "The most important things in life aren't things!" Leaders are funny. We love to create programs and systems and protocols. As staff members and elders at Celebrate! Family Church we continually remind one another that "People are more important than programs". Really, we repeat that "mantra" on a regular basis because we need to always keep in mind that what we do is based on the chief concerns of the Chief Shepherd.

---

[15] Wigglesworth, Smith; "Devotional..."; Whitaker House: 1999; p. 424

Jesus took over six hundred Pharisaical laws and concentrated them into two key concepts: Love the Lord and Love the people (Matthew 22:37-37 Paraphrase). The two priorities for Kingdom living are our relationship with God and our connection with the people around us. When we care about people we endeavor to bless, honor and communicate that value to them. We want to be clear and encouraging, always projecting faith and possibility. The trouble we run into is that often a program we created to serve us can end up becoming a task master demanding that we serve it! One time we established a policy that everyone who served in an "up front" ministry (i.e. obvious to people) should wear a shirt and tie for men. A dress or skirt/blouse was expected for women. Sounds good, looks professional. The problem? We live in a farming community! Shirts and ties are not normal attire. In fact, many of our members don't EVER wear shirts and ties unless they go to church! Some don't even own shirts and ties! So we found ourselves in a dilemma. We had a program that sounded good, but if enforced, excluded a large percentage of the people willing to serve. What did we do? We modified our dress code to express our desire to be nicely dressed in honor of the Lord and to present the church in a spirit of excellence without dictating the specifics of what honorable or excellent dress looks like. We've left the decision as to how to demonstrate honor and excellence in their attire up to those who serve on our teams. Our volunteers know what we're trying to do (demonstrate honor) and why we're trying to do it (model a message of excellence); they don't need their leaders to micromanage their behavior. The message we are sending is "We believe in you AND we trust your judgement".

What hill are you willing to die on?

The question amounts to "What *really* matters?" Whether your involvement is in a family, a business or a ministry the issues of concern must be rated on a sliding scale. A wise person once advised "Beware of majoring in the minors." As members, care-givers and leaders we must be alert to the reality that we often (usually) have strong opinions about our direction, our future and our methods. Visionary leadership demands that that goals be set and plans be refined. The danger arises when we get so smitten with our own ideas and methods that we are willing to roll over the top of the people around us in an effort to see those objectives met.

I often employ the "hill to die on" analogy when counseling and advising families. It is particularly germane to those with challenging teenaged children (all teens will be a challenge to some degree, I think it's a characteristic of their "species"). Teens will test every boundary set for them. It's part of growing up. They are learning the basis of and skills needed to establish their own baselines and norms of behavior. I encourage parents of these guys not to get all hung up on a detail or two. When I was growing up

I deliberately did the opposite of most things my parents told me. Boys have short hair – I grew mine long. Clean neat clothing makes a statement – my most worn out blue jeans were my favorite pants. But, the older I got, the "smarter" Mom and Dad got! I'm at the point now that I sometimes scare myself with the similarities between my parents and myself! This is my point–choose some core values that really matter, which are truly important to you. What really matters to your way of life? Identify things that will truly affect the future potential of your child. Determine "the big deals" in life and hold-on to those expectations. Everything else, unless it's potentially life threatening or debilitating or has irreversible negative possibilities, just let it slide while you watch from the sidelines to discern how things will look as time goes on and as "the teenaged dust settles."

How important are your expectations?

One more area of priority assessment that we can draw and learn from is in the arena of marriage. Prior to the wedding date, during one of my final sessions of premarital counseling, I ask the couple to list their expectations of the covenant partnership they are about to enter together. I ask them to list 25 expectations. Some couples come up with a few more, some identify a few less, but that's a good number to start with. Once they've got their list I ask them to rate their thoughts on scale of One to Three. A priority three is the lowest or least important; it would be nice if this expectation were realized in the relationship but it's not any big deal if it isn't. Level two is pretty important and a valuable future goal to set, but life would still go on without it. A number one is an absolute must – failure in this area is a deal-breaker for the marriage. I've had all kinds of answers and evaluations. A three might be having a new car – it sure would be nice but it's not the most important thing the couple will face. An example of a two on the scale might be owning a home – it's a good goal and one they want to pursue but everybody knows it could take time and might be a bit of a struggle. But every couple and both parties in every couple will rate faithfulness to each other in the marriage as an absolute #1! And rightly so! Without faithful commitment to one another no marriage is going to survive. Here's my point, not everything in the marriage or in life can be a number one! Some things are major, others are not – don't major in the minors!

"You must earn the right to speak into the lives of others"
(Rev. Richard Williams)

These principles of family structure, living and management are true in business and ministry as well. Everything can't be a "drop dead" issue! When I demanded that a bunch of farmers wear shirts and ties to serve on Sunday morning I was majoring in the minors – I created a deal-breaking, number one situation when it would have been better to see that it really is a two or even a three. I have since learned that it's more important that our volunteers, employees and family members get involved than it is that they are "dressed to the nines" while they serve.

No more buts

No one wants to hear the word "but" in a sentence intended to express care, concern or apology. We've all had it happen. Having been wronged in a discussion someone tries to make it right by expressing their remorse for your hurt feelings "<u>but</u> you really upset me with what you said." When "but" is added as the pivot point of a sentence, everything stated prior to "the but" is considered to be empty by the hearer. "I shouldn't have shouted at you '<u>but</u>' you just kept pushing me." "I know I'm late '<u>but</u>' the traffic was terrible."

Don't shoot the messenger! Right now someone is reading themselves into this scenario and realizing this is a problem for them. In fact, it is a problem for most leaders unless they have specifically identified this tendency and they work hard to overcome it. There is a quick and easy solution and it works virtually every time in every situation with every person! (Just send me $100 and I'll tell you what it is! – Relax – I'm Just Kidding!)

Here's the "trick". Simply replace the word "but" with the word "and". Now try the same sentences again. "I shouldn't have shouted at you *and* I'm going to try harder not raise my voice when we're talking." "I know I hurt your feelings *and* I'm really making an effort not to do that anymore." "I know I'm late *and* I apologize, please forgive my tardiness."

An exercise in self-awareness

The leaders in Acts 6 realized that this need was serious to those who had it and responded with an attempt at solution. They essentially said: "This need is valid *and* we need to get somebody who can address it and fix it." The leaders interpreted the presentation of this issue as an exercise in self-awareness not an occasion for self-defense. They chose to approach the challenge as if it were an opportunity for leadership expansion rather than reacting with excuses or with an attempt to deflect responsibility to someone else.

One of the most striking realities of this whole process is that it took place early in the first century AD. There were no leadership websites. No employee awareness workshops. No church growth conferences. The solutions they found were completely organic in that they were motivated and resourced simply by the need that arose, and by the spiritual wherewithal and wisdom of men and women who were determined to find solutions to their problems. The changes made by the local leaders addressed the concerns and brought grass-roots resources to bear on those concerns. They were open to change and leveraged that attitude into excellent care, amazing growth and a fresh approach to leadership expansion.

Second Wind Principles

Read:

The Apostle Paul prays for his friends in the church located in Ephesus that "the eyes of your understanding being enlightened; that you may know what is the hope of His calling, what are the riches of the glory of His inheritance in the saints... (Ephesians 1:18 emphasis added).

Reflect:

The Greek word used for "enlightened" in this passage is the word "photizo" – it is the word from which we derive the English word "photograph" or visible impression. Paul is essentially telling his friends that they need a new mental impression or "mind photo" of themselves relative to God's amazing call, care, provision and power at work in their lives.

Reset:

1. Can you identify any areas of your thinking in which you have harbored or assumed a perspective of

yourself, your life, your calling, your destiny which is less than the reality Paul paints for his friends?

_____

_____

2. Have you given up on any dreams? Which ones? Why?

    _____

    _____

    _____

3. What dreams, destiny or future outcomes would you like to see God revive in your thinking and planning?

    _____

    _____

    _____

Chapter 5

LOCAL LEADERSHIP AND MEMBERSHIP

Acts 6:2 " (...the twelve) summoned the multitude..."

In a Graduate Level Leadership class hosted by Northwest Graduate School of the Ministry in Kirkwood, WA and taught by Dr. John Maxwell, the question was raised: "Are leaders born or made?" Dr. Maxwell, ever the jokester, replied "Well, I've never met a leader who wasn't born!" Both the question and the tongue-in-cheek reply were well-received. What happens when leaders find themselves in circumstances for which they feel ill-equipped and unprepared? It's not unusual to begin questioning whether perhaps the leader's placement was premature or even inappropriate all-together.

Stuff doesn't stay fixed!

I came to pastoral ministry from the world of construction. I've expressed my transition by commenting that I was a general contractor "in a previous life." One thing I've come to appreciate about the construction world is that as a rule once you fix something it stays fixed! In my relationships with people, leadership and ministry I've found that stuff doesn't stay fixed! People are constantly changing which results in a new crop of issues and concerns on an almost daily basis. In my contracting days I owned the company, I bid the jobs, I estimated the materials required, I paid the bills and I collected the money! It was pretty obvious to me and everyone else who was the boss. "Whose name is on the contract?" Mine! That means I'm in charge – Oh to live those simple days again!

My leadership role in local church ministry was inherited when the former pastor of the church died very suddenly and unexpectedly. He had previously asked me if I would agree to help him on a volunteer basis with various projects and leadership needs as my time would allow and while still operating the construction company and I had agreed to serve. Not surprisingly then, at his passing, the leaders of the church approached me and asked if I could "help the church for a while" as they considered how to proceed in the pastor's absence. (This has turned out to be one of the longest "for a while" seasons of my life as I've continued in the pastoral role at that same church for almost twenty-five continuous years!)

My expectations were met with resistance

When I came into the lead role at the church, unbeknownst to me, there were several others in the congregation who had concluded that they, and not I, should be the next lead person. Without going into detail, it is sufficient to say that they made my job very difficult with criticism, alternative perspectives and undermining among the members of the congregation. While I had taken on the duties of pastor with some level of trepidation, I had also taken the responsibility with excitement and an eager curiosity to see how this would all work out for the Kingdom as well as for myself and my family. My expectations and eagerness were soon met with resistance and conflict to the degree that I began to wonder if perhaps I was the wrong man for the job.

The questions of who should lead and why are valid. All of us will encounter times when we will ask ourselves if we are the "right man/woman" for the job. We will likewise, be confronted with the need to consider questions of appropriateness of assignment relative to others in our circles of leadership. Maybe, we think, someone else could do it better. At various times these same questions have become my excuse for failure when faced with difficult or seeming no-win situations. "This wasn't my idea" or "I never wanted this job in the first place" seem like good duck-and-cover phrases when the pressures or the demands seem unmanageable and insurmountable.

"The mighty oak was once a little nut that stood its ground"
(Rev. Tom Brazell)

Too many insecure leaders

In the Acts 6 narrative, it states that "...the twelve (the Apostles) summoned the multitude (the rank and file disciples) ..." (parentheses added). This was not a hit or miss arrangement. They didn't randomly point and call out "I need seven volunteers...you, you and you..." There was a known and pre-described group to whom they could turn for help. They had leadership (Apostles) and they had membership (disciples) from which they could draw insight and assistance. I really like the fact that the leaders, in spite of their being "capital – A" Apostles, did not think themselves too high and mighty to consult with and seek the advice and help of the rank and file members of the group. Too many leaders are insecure and threatened by the fact that there are high-quality members in their ranks, some of whom can do the job as well as or sometimes better than the leader himself. Having great people is not a threat, it is a tremendous blessing and one for which all leaders should strive and be thankful.

The group pulled together

The presentation of this "complaint" caused the whole group to pull together as they sought a reasonable and workable response. They weren't trying to explain the problem away, they were seeking to engage the issue and bring it under control through good management and smart utilization of available people and resources.

The membership roster or the office team can become the "recruitment pool" for new leadership. Often the next manager, team leader or department director is sitting right next to us in the staff meeting! Once the leader can get past their own proud independence and insecurity and see their way clear to invite and trust others to share in the challenges of leading, they often find that the help they so desperately need is already on the team. All that remains is to identify those people and equip them for the work at hand.

What are we looking for?

We'll cover this subject in more depth during Chapter 6 but since this discussion is focused upon looking locally for the next leaders in our organization, we will take a cursory look at leadership qualifications now. The Apostles in our narrative actually delegated the solution to the complaint of the Hellenist widows to representatives of the membership group. In one version of Acts 6 the Apostles task the "disciples" (members) by charging them: "…look around among yourselves, brothers, and select seven men who are well respected and are full of the Holy Spirit and wisdom. We will put them in charge of this business." (Acts 6:3 NLT)

What have the Apostles realized? They've come to understand that they already have the leaders they need; they just have to identify who they are. The task of naming leaders is guided by the characteristics they think will provide for the needs of the group, will represent the current leadership core and will clearly demonstrate the heart of God toward the people. They conclude that they should look for people who are "well respected," "full of the Holy Spirit" and show godly "wisdom" or mature spiritual acumen. If I were writing the search criteria for these new leaders, I would seek people of Character – Dependability – Spirituality – Integrity – Trust.

Look for FAT people!

A friend of mine once told me, "When looking for leaders, I look for FAT people"! He informed me that "FAT people" are: Faithful – Accountable – Teachable. These are essentially the same priorities the Apostles expressed. They are looking for people who are <u>faithful</u> – to the Lord, to His word, to their friends and to their co-laborers. All premarital couples instinctively know that faithfulness to one another is a major (THE major) component in a successful marriage. Furthermore, top-notch people are <u>accountable</u> – they know that they will answer to someone. There is no place for a "loose cannon" on your ministry team, in your leadership group or in trust-based relationships. An important aspect of a persons' role in business or ministry is knowing who is boss. It's popular in today's culture to assert that no one is "over" anyone else. The Scriptures tell us that while we shouldn't "lord over" those in our care, it is imperative that we know and submit to those who are placed over us in our world – whether that be in the personal, business, ministerial or governmental realm (Matthew 20:25; Hebrews 13:17).

The final characteristic of the high-quality leadership candidate is that they are <u>teachable</u>. "A leader is a reader!" Why? Because our God and our people deserve the very best we can offer. We get better, stronger, more astute and more mature when we commit to continual personal growth. "Study to show yourself a workman approved unto God..." (2 Timothy 2:15 KJV) There is no way to reach our full potential without a devotion to continual study. Never stop learning!

"The greater the calling –
The greater the scrutiny before God"
(Os Hillman)

More than superficial knowledge

So, how can we know who has the characteristics needed for a particular leadership role? The Acts 6 leaders admonished the members to "choose from among you." They were advised to seek out the people they needed from among their own ranks – this suggests that they had a more than superficial knowledge of the men and women with whom they worked and related. They were to choose their leaders based on the personal insights and knowledge that they possessed with regard to the "new recruits." How might they have gleaned these insights? My guess is that they continually spent time together in other than church-related business! They knew their strengths and weaknesses. They knew who had compassion. They had identified those who were skilled as communicators and care-givers. They, through relationship, had come to know who was respected in the community. Their depth of knowledge of one another led to the selection of those who had the maturity to face the challenges and meet the demands they would face as they worked to address the needs of large groups of people on a continual basis.

The value of membership

Membership is a demonstration of commitment –

Radio host and psychologist Dr. Laura Schlesinger frequently assesses the depth of a couple's relationship by asking – "Do you have a ring and a date". Her point? Do you have a tangible commitment to each other?

Membership invites accountability –

"FAT people" are willing to show their openness to transparent living. They have decided to allow their leaders access and input into their lives.

- Membership is a tool for organization –
  "...God is not a God of disorder..." (1 Corinthians 14:33 NIV)
  - o Where there is no organization there is confusion
- Membership identifies those who should have a voice in the direction of the group –
  - o We all need to answer the question: "Who has the right to tell me I'm wrong?"
  - o Identifying a core group establishes avenues of trust for meaningful feedback and future growth
- Membership is a step of leadership -
  - o Committed members are the "recruitment pool" for the next generation of leaders
  - o Members set a positive example for others to follow
- Membership opens doors of greater responsibility and ownership –
  - o In the Acts 6 example, the leaders went to the members to find those with the character and qualities necessary to take the "organization" to the next level
- Members can be recommended to others should it become time to move on –

o   When I am able to say "She did a great job for me and I'm sure she'll do the same for you" it becomes a very strong referral for a resume or for future membership in another place.

Membership helps me

When I get a suggestion or a complaint I evaluate the source of that input in terms of relationship. Who should I listen to? Who can I trust to tell me I'm wrong, knowing that their intention isn't to cut me down but to make me and/or my organization better and stronger?

I can't take orders from just anyone – if I do, I won't be leading, I'll be following public opinion.

The Scriptures teach that Jesus "would not commit Himself to them (the general population) because He knew all men" (John 2:24). The irony of this statement is that while He would not give Himself TO them, He was willing to give Himself FOR them! It demonstrates that a leader must couple his/her inner sense of destiny and purpose with an identified core of co-servants in whom he/she can trust before "committing" to any perspective, plan or promise.

> *"The man who wants to lead the orchestra*
> *must turn his back on the crowd"*
> (Max Lucado)

Resistance can be overcome

I mentioned earlier that my Church leadership role came at the sudden loss of our previous Sr. Pastor. The former pastor had been working on a plan to develop both a membership process and a leadership team. When I discovered his plans I thought it would be a good idea to finish what he had started and to implement both groups. It turned out to be one of the major challenges of those early ministry days as the church was about evenly divided into two groups – those who were "for" and those who were "against" the plans. Without going into pages of detail, suffice to say the resistance was overcome and we currently have both a leadership team and a clear path to membership. Both have become tremendous assets for me as a leader.

Membership: an invaluable resource

Our church membership has become invaluable as a "go-to" source and resource:

- Members are who I trust to give me straight-forward evaluation
  - o Membership has produced a safe environment in which to consider "the positive value of negative feedback"
- Members identify themselves through "ownership"

o   I listen for and I've trained our leaders to listen
    for "transition speech." That is, the point at which
    a new attendee stops saying "your church" (<u>your</u>
    church is nice or I like the worship at <u>your</u> church)
    and begins demonstrating personal ownership (I
    love <u>our</u> church, or, when will <u>we</u> begin <u>our</u> hol-
    iday series this year?)

- Members are the group I turn to when I need to find
  more leaders to Raise, Resource and Release into the
  work of the ministry (more on this is in Chapter 6).
- Members are the ones I recruit to lead new
  outreaches.
- Members are our most likely candidates for mis-
  sionary work.

I find it wonderfully encouraging that, just like the
early church, we can get to know and trust our members,
employees and coworkers to the degree that we can recruit
and develop our next "crop" of leaders from within our own
"homegrown stock."

Second Wind Principles

Read:

Behold, how good and how pleasant it is for brethren
to dwell together in unity! It is like the precious oil upon

the head, Running down on the beard, The beard of Aaron, Running down on the edge of his garments. It is like the dew of Hermon, Descending upon the mountains of Zion; For there the LORD commanded the blessing — Life forevermore. (Psalms 133)

Reflect:

That's a lot of strange activity and symbolism for people living in the western world in the 21st Century! I won't try to explain it all I just want to highlight one point. It is so much easier to be "for" one another than against each other. Rev. Joel Osteen points out

> "Oil makes things flow. Whenever there is friction or things get stuck, oil is used to lubricate it and make it more fluid. That is what God is doing with you...things will get easier... people will want to be good to you...you will get (good) breaks...you will have good ideas, wisdom, creativity...that is the oil God is putting on you."[16]

So, what's the point? The point is this: God is working to smooth out the rough spots in our relationships. The

---

[16] Joel Osteen, "I Declare..." pg 105

question He poses to us is – Will we allow Him to bring the peace and mutual trust and submission necessary for true Holy Spirit unity to prevail?

<u>Reset:</u>

1. Who do I need to forgive? Not who needs to apologize to me – God is putting the responsibility on us not upon them!

   _____

2. Begin by asking God to cleanse your own heart of anger, mistrust and bitterness toward:

   _____

3. "Graduate to the next level" by praying a blessing upon and in the life, family, future of:

   _____

Chapter 6

RAISING AND RELEASING MINISTRY LEADERS

Acts 6:3 "Seek out (find) from *among you seven men of good reputation, full of the Holy Spirit and wisdom* that we may appoint over this business."

Christianity isn't passive

Here's a news flash for everyone...Leaders Lead!

"One who thinks he leads when no one follows – is merely taking a walk" (Chinese Proverb)

N otice that the leaders in Verse three <u>did not</u> say—"Find a few folks who don't do anything and aren't busy and let's see if we can get them to help out." Neither God nor we as leaders are looking for people who "won't be missed anyway." They went looking for quality caregivers. They wanted people with character and gifting and a good reputation around town. In essence they were looking for leader candidates who were already leading! Beware of creating a culture of by-standers, people who are content to stand on the sidelines while there is so much kingdom business to be carried out.

The uninvolved are always dissatisfied

Members with no meaningful involvement will stand back and watch you work and serve and give; then you will move on and they will stand around waiting for the next leader to come along and "meet their needs." The cycle can go on for years, meanwhile those same folks will find themselves continually dissatisfied, never rising to live in the anointing and kingdom power to which they have been called. In fact, this very group will often become the ground-zero for the majority of complaint, dissent and dissatisfaction in the organization.

It has been said that there are Three Types of People in the World – There are those who make things happen; There are those who watch things happen; and, There are those who say "What happened!" Leaders are those who make things happen. They are entrepreneurial, they are diligent, they are determined, they are unafraid to make decisions and they are willing to own the consequences of those choices.

"Leadership is unlocking people's potential to become better"
(Bill Bradley)

The "Four R's" of Appointing Leaders:

Recruit –

The leaders in Acts 6 are NOT asking "who do you think we can spare" but "Who is the Holy Spirit calling?" A leader has to be able to hear the "hard call." The people most suited to advancement and leadership roles will be the best our group has to offer. Those whom God calls to Himself will often be the same ones we rely upon every day to help US with OUR assignments! The leaders in Acts 6 saw a bigger picture of God's will and were open to responding to Him at a level that went beyond their own needs, desires and planning.

> "Many believers do not think they are called to full time ministry because they don't feel called to preach on Sunday mornings, but ministry should extend beyond the four walls of the church…Stephen was called to help run the food bank that supplied food to the widows…at first glance it doesn't seem very

spiritual in nature, but Stephen was chosen because he was full of faith and the Holy Spirit...he wasn't chosen to teach or travel or preach and yet God used Stephen mightily..." Keep reading "<u>...Stephen, full of faith and power, did great wonders and signs among the people...and they were not able to resist the wisdom and the spirit by which he spoke</u> [Acts 6:8,10]"

"Stephen was essentially a glorified waiter, but he did not act like a waiter...instead he walked in signs and wonders and brought the influence of the King of kings wherever he went. Those around him were unable to resist that wisdom and the Spirit (he carried) ...Stephen believed he was called to make a difference in his sphere of influence...he took dominion over the area that was entrusted to him and established God's kingdom in Jerusalem...How does the church invade...? Just like Stephen did, **by confidently infiltrating every area of life with the Kingdom of God...**" [17] (Emphasis added)

---

[17] Johnson, Bill with Lance Wallnau; "Invading Babylon – The 7 Mountain Mandate"; Destiny Image, 2013; p.12

God is not looking for expendable people

The text doesn't spell it out, but I'm willing to guess that the men chosen to lead this new area of ministry were already valuable and serving in other parts of the organization. I can't tell you how many times we've been sitting in a leadership meeting discussing an area of needed expansion when the name of a person or couple is brought up for promotion only to have the director of the ministry in which they currently serve silently (or sometimes not-so-silently) release a gasp at the realization of what this transition might mean for their area of service. A "win" for the group may mean a "loss" for you personally!

God calls upon His BEST people NOT His "most expendable" people. He doesn't seek out those who are doing nothing and going nowhere – rather He says: "Separate to Me Barnabas and Saul" e.g. "your two best guys" (Acts 13:2). Recruiting leaders is often relationally costly, personally difficult, corporately demanding!

We respond to the logic of heaven

Successful recruiting demands a good grasp of people and how they function, as well a strong sense of what the Lord and your leadership environment requires. Take a look at this excerpt from "The Seven Mountain Prophecy" by Johnny Enlow:

"We are born with a right brain processor and a left brain processor. That means that the left and right sides of our brain literally process information in an entirely different manner.

Our left brain is verbal and processes info analytically and sequentially... (it works) step by step...(it) is highly organized and likes lists, planning, rules and keeping time...it is logical, sequential, rational, analytical and objective...

Our right brain however, is visual and processes information intuitively and simultaneously. It looks first at the whole picture and then examines the details...the right and left cerebral cortexes are connected by nerve fibers which allow messages to pass between them. The right brain is creative...while the left brain is robotic in accessing whatever is fed into it...Unlike the methodical approach of the left brain, the right brain processes all (of it all) at once. The right brain is not highly organized...it responds by free association. It likes to know the *why*...It is not sensitive to time...it enjoys touching and feeling. It loves patterns, metaphors, analogies, role-playing and visuals...it can be subjective and random...

the right brain listens to *how* something is said (ie inflection & mannerisms).

Upon entering school, most children are predominantly right brain processors and thinkers. It doesn't take long in our education system for that to change dramatically... by the time they graduate from High School more than 98% of kids are left brain dominant...the further they go in education...the more left brain they become...

Most IQ and scholastic aptitude tests measure left brain skills...Our educational system is toxic to the right brain processor causing us to switch from our natural "right brainism" to "left brainism."

Jesus came to a left brain-dominated culture highly influenced by Greek thought – (left brain) rationalism prevailed – God stepped in and said "Repent for the Kingdom of Heaven is at hand" (Mt 4:17).

"Repent" means more than "be sorry for sin" the Greek word "metanoeo" (repent) means to literally "change one's mind, to think differently, to do an 'about face' in one's thinking." With that reality in mind think about this:

"You've been taught that 1 + 1 = 2 and 2 + 2 = 4 but I'm here to tell you that 1 can put a thousand to flight and 2 can chase 10,000.
I'll show you how to feed more than 5000 with 2 fish and 5 pieces of bread – *and to really blow your mind* – you'll have more left over when you're done than you had when you started!
I'm going to cause a blind man to see by putting mud made from spit in his eyes.
I'm going to heal paralytics and forgive sins.
I'm going to speak to storms and they will obey me.
I'm going to defy the laws of physics by walking on water.
Then in the midst of the whole thing – I'll teach you the philosophical opposite of all the (left brain) learning you've received.
If you want to be great you must become nothing; If you want to live you must die; To go up, you must go down...
Then I'll choose twelve backward, volatile, uneducated fishermen and use them as the

antithesis of everything you've been taught to value.

And finally I'll claim my lordship over this world by allowing myself to be brutally beaten, spit at and humiliated so that through my death you all may live...**You'd better meta-noeo now or you just won't get it or get Me or the benefits of the very God who created you**...Your natural mind the way it presently operates is at total odds with Me and what I bring...You can (with left brain) quote all the Scriptures on faith and understand the logic of faith but **only the right brain can tap into the actual substance of faith**...(a huge deal since 'without faith it's impossible to please God' [Hebrews 11:6] and 'Whatever is not from faith is sin'" [Ro 14:23]).

Made in His (Jesus') image **we are wired to respond to the logic of heaven**. We yearn for the supernatural, for the invisible, for the impossible to become possible – for the Kingdom of God...we have been blinded... by being indoctrinated in skepticism, doubt and unbelief...Instead of submitting the right brain to the left brain rationalism, we were created to submit the left brain to right brain (i.e. God-connected) perceptions."[18]

He who says "It cannot be done" should not interrupt him who is doing it!
(Chinese Proverb – Paraphrase)

Speak in faith AND act in faith

Wow! If those thoughts from Johnny Enlow don't get the juices flowing in your faith and feelings – you'd better pause right now and check yourself for a pulse! In order to walk, talk, think and act in the power and with the mindset of God we will have to release ourselves from a traditional, left-brain, (human) logic-based approach to life and leadership. We will need to adopt a Kingdom mentality in both thought AND in practice. We must speak in faith AND we must act in faith. No wonder Jesus reiterated the first Commandment given to Moses:

> 'Hear, O Israel, the LORD our God, the LORD is one. And you shall love the LORD your God with all your heart, with all your soul, with all your mind, and with all your strength." (Mark 12:29-30)

---

[18] Enlow, Johnny; "The Seven Mountain Prophecy..."; Creation House 2008; pp. 85-89; Emphases added

Without a fully functional contingent of all of our mental and physical faculties, all of our awareness and all of our abilities we cannot possibly honor or obey God. Only when we surrender completely to Him can we accomplish His will in our own lives and in the lives of those within our leadership purview.

"You earn your leadership every day"
(Michael Jordan)

Leadership recruitment

A few more thoughts with regard to recruiting. The least effective recruitment tools we can use are the group announcement, the community bulletin board and the bulk handout. These things lack impact because they do not make a personal connection. Here are few recruiting pointers:

- Invite personally, meet them face to face (not Facebook or email)
  - o In the church setting we are often asked to "make an announcement" requesting help or volunteers for some project or plan. I have discovered that the "bulk announcement" is my LEAST effective recruiting tool. I believe the reason for its ineffectiveness lies in the fact that there is no relational contact made in that exchange. In addition, if 100 people hear that there is a need for 5

helpers, they will all look around the room and think "surely they don't need me, with all these people they'll have plenty of help." Interestingly, it is not uncommon to have NO volunteers come forward in answer to a "bulk appeal" for help! Everyone assumes someone else must have volunteered. The result? No one volunteers. Always ask in person.

- Invite your intended new recruit to <u>help</u> you – Say something like: "I've been wondering if you can help me with something" – people like to feel that they are coming alongside. They want to know that their assistance is a blessing and that it will make a difference – they want to lift the load.

- Ask clearly not generally – "I'm leading an usher team on the second Sunday of every month at 10 am and I'd like to invite you to help me on the team." We live in a crazy-busy world in which most people have very little expendable time. To ask someone to commit an unspecified amount of effort for an indistinct length of time is asking them for a blank check on their already very stretched "free time account." A specific request allows them to assess the commitment and draw a valid conclusion regarding their ability to respond to the need. A clear request and a determined response will also cut down on the number of weekly "no-shows" as people get into the ministry and realize they just don't have the time or stamina to meet the demand being placed upon them. With that in mind...

- Specify the term and expectations of the job –
  - o How long is the commitment – 6 months, 1 year, 2 years?
  - o How often will they serve – an hour once per week, month, quarter?
  - o What does the service consist of – holding doors, picking up papers, cleaning?
  - o What time should they report AND when will they be released?
  - o Are there training sessions to attend or leadership meetings required?
  - o What are the benefits – free attendance at special events; early sign up for groups; Our leaders are invited to quarterly meetings with the Sr. Staff and attendance at the annual Staff and Elders Christmas party

Raise –

An anonymous someone once stated "it's lonely at the top." I've had people, attempting to sympathize with what they perceive to be a difficulty in my leadership role, say those exact words to me. In that instance I always want to raise a question – "If it's lonely at the top, why would I want to be there alone?" It is a major mistake for leaders to get so engrossed in what they're doing or the way it "must" be done that they fail to raise the people around them to participate in the performance of the various projects and responsibilities that the leadership role demands.

Many leaders get wrapped up in the notion that their role is one of developing followers. Maybe we want to call them "foot soldiers." They are "boots on the ground." They don't make decisions, they don't call any shots, they just do what they're told. It seems that some leaders prefer this top-down style. In my opinion that directorial approach leads to a lack of ownership on the part of the members. The lack of meaningful involvement opens the door to boredom. People who feel underutilized may begin to wonder "why bother" as they feel less connected. Sadly, many highly capable, potential team members have been left by the wayside because their leaders failed to recognize or employ their gifts and abilities. There are few things more de-motivating for an entrepreneurial, active, forward-thinking person than the realization that they are in a "no-brain" work or service environment.

"True leadership lies in guiding others to success"
(Bill Owens)

Are you raising leaders or followers?

Dr. John Maxwell contrasts those who develop leaders and those who raise up followers in his book "The 21 Irrefutable Laws of Leadership"[19]

LEADERS WHO DEVELOP FOLLOWERS	LEADERS WHO DEVELOP LEADERS
Need to be needed	Want to be succeeded
Focus on weaknesses	Focus on strengths
Develop the bottom 20 percent	Develop the top 20 percent
Treat people the same to be "fair"	Treat leaders individually for impact
Hoard power to themselves	Give power away
Spend time with others	Invest time in others
Grow by addition	Grow by multiplication
Impact only those they personally touch	Impact people far beyond their own reach

A basic formula for raising and training leaders follows:

1 – Learn to accomplish the task with excellence and expertise personally.

2 – Begin taking a future leader along when you perform the desired function.

---

[19] The 21 Irrefutable Laws of Leadership; Maxwell, John C. Nelson Publishing 1998, p 210

3 – Once the protégé has watched and learned, allow them to perform the function while you look on for guidance, support and encouragement.

4 – Release the emerging leader to complete the work on their own without your oversight.

5 – Empower the new leader to take someone along with them and begin the whole process all over again.

Think of it. At the end of one 5-step cycle the leader will have gone from one person doing the work to three people engaged in the effort (the leader, the new leader, the new leader's protégé). After another cycle there will be nine, then twenty seven, then seventy one. This is exponential growth by internal multiplication. It requires trust. It requires a clear picture of what we're doing and why we're doing it. It requires confidence in the people we work with. It requires a continual seeking out of new people to whom we expect to give opportunity and authority in our organization.

Resource –

Raising and resourcing are very time and effort-laden aspects of bringing new leaders on line. Many times, upon asking leaders if they feel equipped for the work, I hear that they feel ill-prepared and somewhat daunted by the task(s) lying ahead of them. Much leadership fails because there is a lack of preparation of the new leaders. It takes more than a job description or an hour in the Director's office to adequately prepare the next generation for leadership.

Dr. Keith Johnson, a professional confidence coach and personal friend, advises pastors that they should only do two things: "Preach great messages" and "Raise up leaders around you." Imagine the growth, stability and effectiveness possible if that multiplying and stabilizing advice were practiced throughout the Christian church world. Astronomical!

Dr. Johnson's coaching further reflects the basic premise that: "The less you do, the more you can accomplish" and "The less you do, the more you can prepare others to fulfill their destiny." The position is quite simply that in order to raise the excellence and efficiency levels while simultaneously growing both the size and intensity of an organization, the primary leaders must maintain a strong and continuous focus on recruiting, raising, resourcing and releasing an on-going flow of fresh leader candidates. It is no threat to existing leadership to "give away power." In fact, the continual release of authority enables fresh ideas and new approaches to begin to take form and to bring new life to the group. In a constantly growing and energizing environment, stagnated, lack-luster or status-quo performance will never be an issue.

A leader must delegate

As previously alluded, in order to adequately resource new leaders, the current regime must be willing to delegate some of its authority to the new crop of fresh leadership. The question will arise as to how this should be done with reasonable caution while still providing an opportunity for implementation of bold and perhaps untested ideologies.

Following is a Three Level Delegation Plan – all three of the levels must be employed for successful delegation to occur. The aspects are represented by three "A-words": Assignment – Authority – Accountability. Use this three-fold strategy for every delegated task in your purview. It will grow your team numerically. You will find that new leaders have a fresh sense of ownership and determination. It will expand the scope of your authority without micro-managing those assigned to take on the new leadership tasks. And here's the really good news: It will simplify your job! You will find yourself less bogged down with details and mentally freer to pursue the next aspect of vision development required by your leadership role. Let's "unpack" the three "A's"

Assignment:

The task ahead should be clear and concise. Any expectations of the job should be communicated to the new leader ahead of time. Allow opportunity for questions or a feedback "loop" to insure that they understand your instructions. Make sure that any guidance or materials needed will be made available to them. If formal approval is required to move forward, make sure they know who to talk to. Care should be taken to pre-evaluate the capabilities of the assignee. Few things are more hazardous to employee relations than a scenario where the emerging leader feels that they have been "thrown into the deep end of the pool without being taught how to swim". The Acts chapter six passage specifies: "Seek out (or find or choose) **from among you...**"

The men chosen to serve were not "unknown quantities." They were known among the leaders and in the community at large. They had already demonstrated a propensity to lead and a level of character that allowed the whole group to recognize and support their appointment. It is advisable to have a probationary or a warm-up period during which the new employee or volunteer or member is observed and has become known to the leaders and to the other team members. There may be prerequisite training. Perhaps a background-check or a security clearance or a drug test is required. Personal and professional relationships will be better and stronger when adequate time and effort have been expended to assure that the right people are being placed in the proper roles.

__Authority__:

    Several years ago we were rolling out a new Children's Ministry curriculum for our Sunday morning gathering. We'd planned for a couple of months, talked it up among our leaders and members, and announced the new date as the first weekend after Labor Day. Excitement flooded the place. We were all eager to have our children experience this fresh approach to Kid's Church. Finally, the big day arrived. As was my habit I arrived at the church early on Sunday and after a few minutes of settling in, turning on lights, unlocking doors, etc. I went looking for the Children's Minister. Upon finding him I said something like "Well, are we all set for today?" It was intended as more of a rhetorical statement than an actual question. He got a sheepish look on his face to which I asked if there was some problem. He informed me that we were not ready as the curriculum had not arrived in time...our start date would be delayed by at least 2 weeks. I was NOT happy! All the ads, promo, talking it up, inviting, excitement — for nothing! As calmly as I could I asked what happened and was informed that because he had been on vacation and then I had been on vacation, the curriculum had not been ordered in time to make our launch date. Did I mention I was NOT happy? Rather than lose it right then and there, I went back to my office to think about how to handle the situation. Upon closing the door, I "heard a Voice" in my head say — "This is your fault you know"! My fault! Why is it my fault? To which the "Voice" said – "why would you trust this leader with the precious souls of all these children but you didn't have the confidence to release him to spend the two hundred dollars he needed to get the curriculum in place?" You see, at that time every expenditure had to be approved by me personally and since we had been on alternating vacations that year the approval had not happened. I mentioned I was NOT happy, right? After calming down for a few minutes I realized that my policy of personally approving expenditures was limiting the flow and the productivity of the leaders around me. I needed to release the authority necessary for my staff to do their jobs without my micro-management. That policy was changed at our next leaders meeting and I am pleased to say no such failure has occurred since. Once a leader has been tasked with an assignment, the corresponding authority to carry out that work must be granted.

"The Bible is like deodorant – It must be applied"
(Margaret Stunt – Hillsong Church – Sydney, Australia)

Let's close the discussion on the release of authority with a few final thoughts. One of the most de-motivating (and potentially work-stopping) scenarios the leader candidate can face is having to perform at an expected level without having been given the preparation or resources to complete the job at hand. Most of us want to solve the problems before us. Those solutions are elusive if not altogether impossible unless we are allowed to make the decisions, acquire the materials, spend the money or hire the personnel necessary to get the project done. When the assignment is given make sure the assignee knows the scope of the work as well as the resources available to them. They should also be versed in the procedure required for the procurement of the assets necessary to accomplish the objective. Is there a budget? How do they access the money? What if they anticipate a budgetary overrun? Is there any staffing available? Who else knows how to do the job and are they available for consultation? The more autonomy we give a leader the more ownership and personal investment they will likely demonstrate.

Accountability:

Autonomy is balanced with accountability. To be accountable is to be able to explain the rationale for a decision, the process used to arrive at the decision and the projected outcome of the decision relative to the goals that have been set. It has been stated already but bears repeating: Do not micro-manage! If you must suggest or correct in the midst of the project do so through a "buy-in" process. Use a variation of the three step problem-solving method discussed earlier (What's the problem? What are the options? What do you think we should do?). The ideal outcome is that the senior leader draws the new leader into the evaluation process with the intention of getting the new leader to identify the issues, the possibilities and the best path to success. The value of a "buy-in" model is that it allows the assignee the opportunity to make in-course adjustments to the plan under the guidance of the senior leader without losing ownership of the project. In addition, the evaluation skills utilized in the problem-solving process will translate to the remedying of other areas of challenge as they arise in this and in future projects. The accountability "loop" should be reviewed with the assignee regularly. As skill, maturity and experience are gained the reviews will be less frequent but should still be maintained.

"Don't expect what you don't inspect"
(Louis V. Gerstner Jr.)

That sound and insightful advice holds true for the delegation of responsibility, its corresponding authority and the need for each of us to be accountable for our decisions and actions.

Release –

"(Seek out) men of good reputation, full of the Holy Spirit and wisdom...appoint them..." As previously observed the Acts 6 narrative does NOT have the Holy Spirit saying: "send me that guy over there who never does anything, won't tithe, doesn't volunteer, can't teach and hates to serve – you'll never miss him anyway." The passage DOES say in essence: "give Me your frontrunners – the gospel power-houses, the men and women who never give up and just won't quit – your biggest givers, your best servants, your most excellent people – Hand *them* over and let Me turn *them* loose on the world!"

Face it, we have all had people we would like to see attend, serve, give, complain, create challenge elsewhere – I have found myself asking God to remove a few folks over the years – a kind of "send them anywhere but here" prayer. Maybe you've prayed that prayer a time or two!

"If it doesn't work at home, don't export it!"
(Anonymous)

We look for leaders who practice what they preach. Some might say, that they "walk the talk." If someone is leading a Men's group focused on integrity or there is a women's group teaching prayer, it is very important to me as a releasing leader that those group leaders are actually practicing the tenets of faith that they are teaching. I once asked a men's group leader "does your wife think you're the best man for this job?" Interestingly, the wife felt there were some glaring inadequacies in the way things were going at home so my advice was "why not get some help, make some adjustments and come back to lead this group with integrity and character and proven performance".

The "Jesus method" for recruiting leaders

I've found that the four "R's" of appointing leaders (Recruit, Raise, Resource, Release) open fresh doors of possibility for new leaders in addition to providing an avenue of training and further equipping for those already engaged in some level of leadership. Remember, all leaders must be teachable (2Timothy 2:15). The willingness to hear and to heed corrective advice is a huge indicator for future potential and growth in an aspiring leader.

The "Jesus method" of recruiting utilizes a very similar four-level plan to take people from by-stander to volunteer to leader. Consider two passages from the Gospel of Matthew:

"Jesus...saw two brothers, Simon called Peter, and Andrew his brother, casting a net into the sea; for they were fishermen. Then He said to them, 'Follow Me, and I will make you fishers of men.' They immediately left their nets and followed Him." (Matthew 4:18-20)

"Go therefore and make disciples of all the nations, baptizing them in the name of the Father and of the Son and of the Holy Spirit, 20 teaching them to observe all things that I have commanded you..." (Matthew 28:19-20)

Watch the pattern in action:

- Recruit: Jesus saw two brothers...(come and)..."follow Me..." (Strong's NT #3694 – "fall-in behind me")

- Raise: "I will <u>make</u> you" (Strong's NT #4160 – appoint, raise up, ordain)
- Resource: "They...<u>followed</u> Him" (Strong's NT #190 – to be in the same way [as])
- Release: (Now you) Go...and make disciples of all nations (the whole world) ..."

The Back Story

Let's think a little bit about what might be the back story for the Acts 6 narrative. Dr. Eugene Peterson in his classic vernacular Bible transliteration "The Message" renders Acts 6:3 thusly -

"...friends, choose seven men...whom everyone trusts... full of the Holy Spirit and good sense...we'll assign them to this task. Meanwhile we'll stick to our assigned tasks..."

As mentioned in chapter one the church, by this time in history, had grown to something in excess of 10,000 members. At this point in the story, the decree has gone out – "go find seven men." Our study is based on the finding and placing of those men along with the aspects of leadership employed and the lessons we can learn and apply to our own twenty-first century responsibilities. But think about this. They have 10,000 people and they need seven leaders. That means they have roughly 9, 993 members who WERE NOT chosen!

I don't know, call me crazy, but people being what they are, I'm thinking there was a little bit of jealousy and maybe some grumbling that went on in the "ranks" once this decision came down. I reflect on Jethro's instructions to Moses in much the same way.

"Select from all the people... (leaders) and place them as rulers of thousands, hundreds, fifties and tens" (Exodus 19:21 Parenthesis added.)

> "To be right with God has often meant
> to be in trouble with men"
> (A.W. Tozer)

I can hear it now – "Why should Sol get a thousand when I get a measly ten? He probably thinks he's better than the rest of us!" I imagine it could have played similarly in the Book of Acts. "Stephen chosen, again? What am I chopped liver?" (pronounced "liv-uh"). Ambition can be a deal breaker when seeking those who will serve humbly as our next generation of leaders.

Regardless of the arena, the primary role of leadership always involves the service of others. In the case of the church it's service for God and service of our fellow members. In the instance of a workplace it could be service of the boss or the employees or the corporation. At any rate, the whole concept of service has at its core a certain level of self-deprecation. There must be a willingness to "lay down one's life for his friends" (John 15:13 NIV).

The raising and releasing of new leaders is one of the main responsibilities of the leader. To do it effectively we must lose any sense of personal "clinginess," whether to the people and their personal value to our efforts or to the authority of our role and our reluctance to share it with others. We must learn to see in terms of the big picture for the group, the organization or the ministry. Correspondingly we must be willing to make decisions that serve the long-term interests of the group. We must be ready to face the fact that what is best for the group may not be what is necessarily the easiest, the most convenient or the most expedient for ourselves.

No one starts out at the top

Consider this observation from Pastor Joel Siegel:

> "A person will never change *the* world until they are willing to change *their* world. The ministry of helps is both the refining pot and the launching pad for the believer who wants to be great for God. He said '...pick out seven men...full of the Holy Spirit...' all seven of these men served faithfully in the ministry of helps. At least two of them, Stephen

and Philip, were later promoted to preaching ministries and were mightily used of God...No one ever starts out in the fullness of his or her ministry. All must begin by proving themselves faithful in the ministry of helps for an extended season...How long is that season? As long as God sees fit (we're talking years NOT weeks or months!)...all should be willing to serve wherever God directs for as long as God chooses...Many Christians are too picky regarding their place of service within the local church...God knows our talents and strengths but He will often assign us to begin serving in a place we would consider to be beneath our true abilities...not to demean us but to help develop our character and test our faithfulness. Those who get mad at the pastor for failing to recognize their gifts do not realize that they have just failed a test set before them by God!"[20]

---

[20] Siegel, Joel; "Assembled Together..."; Castle Rock CO: Big God Media / Siegel Ministries Inc. 2014; pp117-120

Do you trust Him?

Perhaps you are choosing leaders or maybe you have been chosen to lead. And what if you are one of those who has been chosen to lead in a less-than-glamorous role? What if you are one of the seven called to "wait on tables"? Really? That's it? "I've been a member here for five years, I've been tithing for three years, I sing in the choir for Easter...but you want me to be what...a waiter? Well, I never!" Remember the words of the Lord "I know the thoughts I think about you...thoughts of peace and not of evil, to give you a future and a hope" (Jeremiah 29:11).

> *"A great leader can take people where they*
> *don't want to go but really need to be"*
> (First Lady Rosalynn Carter)

The New International Version of the Bible says that He has "plans to prosper you..." We are all inclined to watch out for ourselves, we seek to better our position, we try to leverage ourselves into what we perceive to be the best possible scenario for our future outcome. But often we fail to know the bigger picture. We are not in the position to see the beginning from the end. The devotional writer observes, "The multitude chose seven men to serve tables...but we see that God soon had a better plan for two of them – Philip and Stephen...man chose them to wait tables, but God chose them to win souls...if you are faithful in the humblest role, God can fill you with His Spirit, make you a chosen vessel for Himself, and promote you to a place of mighty ministry... Nothing is impossible to a (person) filled with the Holy Spirit..."[21] Do you trust Him?

A harvest of blessing awaits

Raising leaders is costly. Financially. Relationally. Administratively. We don't send out our least helpful, our least involved or the minimally committed. We send out the very best we have to offer and that will cost us. We have to train new people. We have to re-do that which we have already done. We need a fresh level of patience and zeal and drive and vision. In the end the Scriptures teach "we will reap if we do not faint" (Galatians 6:9). A harvest of blessing awaits those who invest themselves in others with an eye toward the bigger picture of growing the lives and abilities of those around us while simultaneously advancing the purposes and the future of the organization as a whole.

> *"No man will be a great leader who*
> *wants to do it all himself"*
> (Andrew Carnegie)

---

[21] Wigglesworth, Smith; Daily Devotional; Whitaker House, New Kensington PA, 1999; p.133

Second Wind Principles

Read:

Let no one despise or think less of you because of your youth, but be an example (pattern) for the believers in speech, in conduct, in love, in faith, and in purity. (1 Timothy 4:12 Amplified Bible)

Reflect:

This is an interesting passage. On one hand Timothy is advised essentially to stand up for himself. "Let no one think less of you…" But as Paul unpacks the "tools" young Timothy is to use in his "self-defense" we find that he is to use unconventional (for our culture) "weaponry." He wins this argument not by physical prowess in the boxing ring but by modeling and demonstrating, and by being an example and godly pattern for others to follow.

Reset:

1. What limitations in your life have held you back from attaining your full calling in the things of God?

_____

_____

2. In what ways have you limited the forward potential in those around you (co-workers, children, spouse)?

_____

_____

3. Who can you help to rise to a fuller realization of their true place in the plan God has for them?

_____

_____

4. How can you be a better, stronger example for those whom you lead or serve?

_____

_____

Chapter 7

FOCUSED PURPOSE

Acts 6:4 "...we will give ourselves continually
to prayer and the ministry of the word..."

D r. Eugene Peterson asserts that the Apostles released new leaders to meet the pastoral care needs of the group while they reaffirmed the demands of their own calling: "we'll stick to our assigned tasks..." (Acts 6:4, The Message). It doesn't sound like reluctant resignation to an undesirable role nor does it sound, from previous discussion, that the leaders are just trying to "ditch" the Hellenistic widows to get them off their backs. They have expressed genuine heart-felt care for the women AND articulated the need to answer the call that God has placed upon their own lives.

Houston we have a problem!

Someone once shared that when pastors were asked as to the nature of their true calling almost all of them stated that they were called to "equip the saints for works of service" (Ephesians 4:11-12). When the same question of pastoral calling was directed to the members of those churches, most of the members replied that the work of the pastor was to "meet the needs of the people." Houston, we have a problem! The people have concluded that the pastor works to serve and care for them and the pastors have concluded that they have been instructed to get the people to go to work!

"Do something every day that scares you"
(First Lady Eleanor Roosevelt)

It is vitally important that leaders and their protégés have a clear picture of the calling to which they have responded. Many needless arguments and damaging interactions result from the lack of "role clarity." Listen to the writer of the Book of Proverbs speak about the value of vision and clarity:

Where there is no vision [no redemptive revelation of God], the people perish; but he who keeps the law [of God, which includes that of man] —blessed (happy, fortunate, and enviable) is he. (Proverbs 29:18 Amplified Bible)

Articulating a redemptive revelation

The vision we have as leaders is more than a preferred picture of the future – it is a "redemptive revelation." Our direction is not random nor is it simply our personal preference. Consider the historical church's record of service and sacrifice which includes even the martyrdom of its leaders and followers. I'm sure that each of them had a "personal preference" that did not include whatever horrible fate to which they were eventually submitted. But their perception of purpose was bigger than their sense of personal preference. It was wider in scope and plumbed deeper depths than their goals for their own lives. They were focused on a greater cause. Looking forward to a "better covenant...established on better promises" (Hebrews 8:6). They knew that in order to be "blessed, happy, fortunate and enviable" (Amplified Bible) the vision they lived, promoted and taught must be God-sized and not simply man-sized. They were ready to live out the reality of the passage that says "with men this is impossible but with God all things are possible" (Matthew 19:26). These men and women were willing to get outside of their own possibilities and enter into the (humanly) impossible realm of God's amazing grace and goodness.

"Leadership is the ability to translate vision into reality "
(Warren Bennis)

Find your place in His redemptive purpose

When endeavoring to lead, whether in the church or elsewhere, what we opt NOT to do can be of equal or more importance than the things we choose to do. Our decision is not based upon our personal preference for one task over another. Our choices are directed by the realization that God has a specific plan in place and that each of us has a distinctive part to play within that plan. Each of us must find the aspect of His redemptive purpose to which we have been assigned. The men in Acts 6 knew what they needed to do (provide for the widows) AND what they needed to NOT do (leave their calling to "serve tables" Acts 6:2). Though the line is often a hard one to draw, what we choose NOT to do will often clear the way for that which we SHOULD do!

"In periods where there is no leadership society stands still"
(Pres. Harry S. Truman)

It must be noted that the apostles did not say that the tables should not be served, only that *they* were not the ones who should do the serving. Again note, it was not because they didn't care or that they were "above" serving tables, but because they had other assignments to which they were specifically and divinely called.

As we learn and grow we gain the insight that it is "God who works in you (us) both to will and to do His good pleasure"

(Philippians 2:13 Parenthesis added). A leader friend of mine when challenged on a decision will frequently reply "I have no horse in this race." He's simply clarifying that the outcome being faced is not specifically his own idea or even necessarily his preference, but he is responsible to make decisions and choices that provide for the greater good of the organization he leads as well as providing for the care and growth of those who are members of that group.

What should you be doing?

Someone asked me "What are you doing that only you can do?" You see, it comes down to making the hard call that some things must be done and others must be deliberately and personally left undone. The leader must make allowance for time, for prayer, for consideration and for getting the counsel needed to define and implement that which he/she should be doing. Everything that does not fit into the category of what must be done by the leader must either be forgone or delegated to someone else.

Tony Hsieh, founder and CEO of Zappos.com, a major on-line merchandiser famous for its customer service and consumer satisfaction, adds balance to this discussion in an observation from his 2010 book "Delivering Happiness." While sharing some of the growth pains and challenges he faced as Zappos began to expand, Tony says "We initially considered outsourcing our call center to overseas providers...

but we remembered...*Never outsource your core competency*...(since) we were trying to build our brand to be the best in customer service, we knew we shouldn't outsource *that* department" (Italics added).[22] Having a focused purpose and keeping an eye on our desired outcome especially during stress or pressure will allow continued forward movement while recognizing areas that need to be strengthened, dropped or delegated.

Who decides what to do?

So who decides what we must and must not do? In the Acts 6 scenario the leaders had the sense that the decision was actually made by God Himself so it was a fairly simple choice from that perspective. If God was telling them to exegete the word and preach, then because of the time and focus that task involves, they concluded He must not be calling them to serve the tables. It's important here to reiterate that while they themselves were not to wait on tables, it was their responsibility as leaders to see that the tables and the people at those tables were taken care of.

> *"Failing to plan is planning to fail"*
> (Rev. Ruth Rodriguez)

---

[22] Hseih, Tony; "Delivering Happiness..."; Hachette Book Group, New York, 2010; p.130

The decision to do or not do certain things may be a matter of organizational by-laws or a job description or some other pre-written document. In those cases, the decision is mostly made for us. Often, however, the choices of the do's and don'ts are left to the leader. Sometimes there are pre-sumed "job requirements" for no other reason than the previous leader did things a particular way or had areas of specific gifting. These expectations can be hard to break especially if the former leader was well-liked or especially effective. Regardless of the circumstances, the ability to "give ourselves" to certain tasks while avoiding others is one of the keys to effective, efficient and excellent leadership. It is one aspect of leadership that cannot be assigned, delegated or outsourced. Each leader must face these decisions for themselves.

"We worked to build trust..."

In a recent interview, Yang Yuanqing, the new CEO of Lenovo, currently ranked #1 in global PC sales, made this observation regarding the decisions the company made while still in their corporate infancy –

> "Back then we made trust our first priority. Many companies emerging from China at that time were not trustworthy, they just wanted to make money...we did whatever we could to build trust in the company...no

matter what we sold to a customer, we made sure it was a good product...we made sure we delivered results on whatever our sales-people had promised to the customer."[23]

The best way a leader can "deliver results" to people is to remember and maintain the focus of his or her role not only in the business or ministry, but in the larger concern of the needs, expectations and promised outcomes for others involved with that leader.

Get beyond "common thinking"

People ask all the time "How can I know the will of God" or "What is my purpose"? In the Book of Romans the Apostle Paul writes "Do not be conformed to this world but be trans-formed by the renewing of your mind..." (Romans 12:2) If Paul were to join us in the 21st century and was posed the "How do I know the will of God" question he would most likely answer: "Don't be limited by conventional or common or circumstantial thinking...Don't be conformed to the way you've always done things...But be changed. Be reconfigured in your thinking. Get a new mindset with regard to life and work and leadership...". Romans 12:2 draws a conclusion: "**Then** you will be able to test and approve what God's will

---

[23] Hvistendahl, Mara; "Lenovo – An interview with Yang Yuanqing"; Delta Sky Magazine, January 2016; p.60

is — his good, pleasing and perfect will." (NIV – emphasis added). The Apostle has made a vital connection: "If you will DO the Word of God, then you will be IN the will of God." An uncommon God takes us to more than common levels.

Do you think you can or do you think you can't?

A Hebrew proverb advises that "As a man thinks in his heart, so is he..." (Proverbs 23:7). A modern day speaker might say: "As you believe you will begin to behave". Many years ago I attended a secular leadership seminar during which the program moderator made the statement – "Whether you think you can or you think you can't...you're right!" Honestly, I don't remember anything else she said that day but that one statement has been a part of my thinking ever since. If we aspire to believe and to achieve the things God has set before us, the biggest change we will have to make is right between our own ears! We will need our mind reconfigured and "transformed" to align with His plan, His promises and His provision. In His presence our thinking is clarified and our actions begin to align with His plan. In this environment people begin to see, to feel, to appreciate and to trust the call of the Lord. Fresh confidence is born for the direction we are traveling and for the outcome we are anticipating.

"If you're going nowhere any road will get you there"
(Anonymous)

The leaders in our study didn't see the Hellenistic widows as a problem to avoid but as a human detail to be cared for as they developed their core leadership and their corporate priorities. They believed the "complaint" was valid and acted promptly to bring an amicable solution through the release of more leaders to meet the demand. Tony Hsieh, regarding Zappos' continued expansion says that they are "constantly improving the customer experience while simultaneously strengthening our (corporate) culture." (Parenthesis added)[24] If we, as leaders, are to serve and grow in our business or ministry, we must remain open to the guidance of the Lord in the development and reinforcement of our primary focus. We must stay in touch with the reasons for doing what we do. We must continually develop our outreach while never ignoring our in-house issues or the needs and concerns of our personnel.

The shortest distance between two points!

Years ago a friend pointed out that contrary to the conclusions of Archimedes – "Sometimes the shortest distance between two points is a U-turn!" If I'm driving north in the state of Virginia and my destination is Florida, I must come to a painful admission – "Oh no – I'm going the wrong way!" The shortest, quickest way for me to get my life straightened out

---

[24] Hsieh, Tony; "Delivering Happiness..."; p.230

at that moment is to find the nearest place to make a U-turn so I can begin traveling in the right direction. Wayne Cordeiro, in his book "Leading on Empty" says "When depression hits, look at your divine commission and say 'This is where I need to start (over) again'."[25] It is telling that Wayne stipulates "when depression hits" not "if depression hits." I once heard Bill Hybels at a conference in central New York make the statement, "There's going to be a train wreck." He was talking about trying to live – business as usual – when all the signs around us are saying something needs to change. Bill's con-clusion was that we should "schedule our own train wrecks" with the Lord in order to allow Him access and opportunity to make the adjustments He has in mind for our lives.

Are you going in circles?

Dr. John Maxwell likes to say "If you always do what you've always done, you'll always get what you've always gotten." A friend of mine says, "If you keep seeing the same scenery, you're going in circles!" Leaders don't have the time to repeatedly do ineffective things or to expend their energy by going in circles. Leaders are those who need to main-tain their focus on the vision and their role in attaining it. When leaders get thrust into a new situation they look it over, they pray, they study, they examine their options, they

---

[25] Cordeiro, Wayne; "Leading on Empty..."; Bethany House, 2009; p.200

ask for outside opinions and help – then they make a plan and take action – usually by recruiting, raising and releasing other leaders to take on some of the responsibility with commensurate authority. Meanwhile those leaders will "knuckle down" and be even more committed and devoted to the demands, the tasks and the role that only they are equipped to lead and to manage.

> *"Lion or bear...I killed it–and I'll do*
> *the same to this Philistine pig..."*
> (King David – 1 Samuel 17:36 – The Message)

How to Know God's Focused Purpose for Your Life

1. What is your PASSION?

   What incites you; enrages you; excites you; keeps you awake at night; makes you cry?

   What is the Holy Spirit speaking into your heart and mind? (Hint – it'll be more than "don't forget the mortgage payment!") God's plan will be big! His plans are bigger than we are! His plan for us is intentionally so big that we cannot attain it without His help.

2. What are God's PROMISES to your life?

   What does the Word of God say about your passions and interests? Watch out for weirdness!

   Someone told me their Spiritual Gift was "I know when people are going to die!"

- Where do we find that particular gift in the Bible? I haven't seen it!

  Your purpose in God will come straight from His word. Your purpose will be a Biblical purpose!

  Use tools to help you research, study and discover His best for you. Don't hesitate to use a Concordance, a Bible Dictionary or an On-line Bible site. Actively seek the counsel of a theologically and spiritually mature friend or leader. This is an important process, do all you can to make it as productive as possible.

3. What is your PURSUIT?

   What steps are you willing to take to answer and respond to your purpose?

   The Apostles in Acts 6 said "We will GIVE OURSELVES" (to prayer and the ministry of the Word)

   To what are you willing to GIVE YOURSELF? Is it a Biblical calling? Is it affirmed by the Holy Spirit and solid, mature Kingdom members?

Excellence honors God

"We must fight for excellence because it is excellence that honors God. It is excellence that inspires people. And it is excellence that means trouble for the enemy of our souls... everything I do in Christian leadership – every plan I put together, every meeting I lead, every talk I give – needs to be my...very best offering! Not so that I'll operate out of paranoia or wild perfectionism, but so that I'll live from my heart's deep desire to honor God...I wonder what would happen to every church on the planet if every pastor, staff member, volunteer, elder or deacon, and servant in children's ministry were to say 'you don't have to worry about me. I'm committed to giving my best...every single day. I'm going to live in vital union with God, and I'm going to consistently render my most excellent offering. The standard I have set for my self is higher than any you could possibly set for me!"[26]

Now, *THAT* is excellence and faithfulness to God's calling!

Stay on the leading edge

We are to remain focused AND we are to pursue God's best while simultaneously offering our own best throughout the entire process. Someone said "If it was easy anybody could do it"! Truer words have not been spoken when it comes to staying on track and on top in the world of business and in the world of ministry. In fact, in any realm of "people

---

[26] Hybels, Bill; "Axioms..."; Zondervan; Grand Rapids MI, 2008; pp.207-208

service" the need to stay on the leading edge of continual care and connection is vital to the ongoing vision, mission and expansion of that work. At times we may feel overwhelmed. We may wonder if we can stay with the plan. There may be an underlying concern that if we do stick it out we'll be worn down to the point of having sacrificed ourselves – mentally, physically, relationally – for the cause at hand.

"...for a dream comes with much business and painful effort...
(Ecclesiastes 5:2 – The Amplified Bible)

Don't we know it! But listen! Your dream is worth your best effort. Stay focused, pursue excellence, hang on to that dream and never give up – your second wind is coming!

Second Wind Principles

Read:

"...one thing I do, <u>forgetting</u> those things which are behind and reaching forward to those things which are ahead, I press toward the goal for the prize of the upward call of God in Christ Jesus." (Philippians 3:13-14)

Reflect:

The Greek definition of this word "forgetting" does not mean "failing to remember." There are some things that we will never forget in that way. Bad things have happened, loved ones have passed on, changes have occurred whether pleasant or otherwise. People don't "fail to remember" those things. This usage of "forgetting" literally means "no longer controlled by." Look at who is making the statement. He is the same one who "did not fail to remember" that "...from the Jews five times I received forty stripes minus one. Three times I was beaten with rods; once I was stoned; three times I was shipwrecked; a night and a day I have been in the deep..." (2 Corinthians 11:24-25). The reiteration of the account goes on but the point is already made – Paul has not forgotten in the traditional sense; he has simply made the decision not to let past struggles hinder God's plans for his future or for the awesome destiny being sketched out before him.

Reset:

1. What things from your past have hindered your sense of possibility for the future and your personal destiny?

_____

_____

2. What needs to happen for you to be released ("no longer controlled by") those overshadowing experiences?

_____

_____

3. Dreams I have for the "new, no-longer-controlled me":

_____

_____

Chapter 8

CONTENTMENT

Acts 6:5 "The saying pleased the whole group..."

I have, at times, referred to this dynamic in the early church as "content–ability". In other words, it is the ability to be content. They were willing to be satisfied. We live in a discontented world. People seek to change everything from their looks to their location. A friend of mine is quite thin, in fact I think he's one of those folks about whom it is said "he doesn't have an ounce of fat on his body." He frequently laments that no matter how much he eats he just can't gain weight. I'm one of those people who wish they could know what that was like for even a couple of weeks! It seems that if I look at food I gain weight. It's the old adage: the girls with the curls want straight hair and the straight-haired girls want the curly hair. No matter where we are or what we have, we want to be somewhere other than here and have something other than this.

Everyone wants something more

What is it with the human element? No matter what we have, we always seem to want something more. Isn't this exactly what happened in the Garden of Eden?

> "Of every tree in the garden you may freely
> eat; but of the tree of the knowledge of good
> and evil you shall not eat..." (Genesis 2:16-17).

Adam and Eve had free run of the whole place and were allowed to do anything they wanted *except* eat from this one tree – so what tree do they decide to eat from? Right! The only one forbidden them!

A friend of mine is a drag racing enthusiast. In a recent conversation he was regaling me with drag race trivia. He surprised me with one detail in particular. He said "You know that drag racers no longer run on a quarter mile track, don't you?" Which, of course, I did not know. He explained that most of the drag strips were built during the muscle car days of the late 50's, 60's and early 70's. In those days a fast car could go somewhere close to 150 mph in a quarter mile. Consequently, all the drag tracks are built to allow for accelerating *and stopping* a vehicle traveling plus or minus 150 mph. While that seems pretty fast to me, racers have pressed for more speed. Along with that pursuit and its' conquest, has come an unforeseen challenge.

The drag tracks can handle cars traveling 150 mph but today's cars are capable speeds in excess of 300 mph! The issue of speeding up has become much less of a concern than the problem of slowing down! The tracks of yesteryear don't allow enough run-off distance to stop the new cars at the end of the race. Thus, the decision was made to shorten the track to 1000 feet thereby slowing the time allowed for acceleration by a small amount. The shortened distance was intended to allow the extra track length needed to safely decelerate at the end of the run. This worked for a short time. Though my friend reports that since the time the tracks were shortened, mechanical and technical advances in the last few years have enabled the newer cars to still exceed 300 mph! Even with the track shortened by almost 25% the push for more has taken the industry past any previously recognized milestone. And they're still working to go faster!

The point is this, we are human beings! We always want more! We are virtually never happy with any decision, any victory or any accomplishment. The first man and woman could have anything they wanted EXCEPT the fruit from the one tree the Lord specified. Skinny people want to be heavier. Heavy people want to be skinnier. No matter how fast a car can go – someone will always want it to go faster.

Discontentment is built into our world

Biblically speaking, it is not uncommon to find that a basic level of discontentment is, to some degree, built into our world:

> "There are three things that are never satisfied, Four never say, "Enough!": The grave, The barren womb, The earth that is not satisfied with water—And the fire never says, "Enough!" (Proverbs 30:15-16)

While these discontented "four" are not people per se, they do belie a certain similarity to humans in that as a species it seems we always want more. It's really not all that surprising that Adam and Eve chose to pursue the one thing they were disallowed. Achan had all the promises of "a land flowing with milk and honey" before him but sacrificed his own life and the lives of his entire family by taking the one thing forbidden him, the spoils of the city of Jericho (Joshua 7:19ff). King David had a great life and an incredible walk with the Lord but wanted his general's wife badly enough to have the man killed rather than have his own covetousness and adultery revealed (2 Samuel 11:1ff). Not only are we not satisfied, but we are willing to go to great, even self-destructive lengths to further the accumulation of our possessions, resources and accomplishments.

If only they had trusted God

People in general, during personal assessment, have a tendency to magnify and multiply the severity of their problems while at the same time we tend to minimize or even nullify our own potential, our possibilities and the impact of God's promises in response to those personal challenges. Remember the report of ten out of twelve spies sent into the land of promise:

There we saw the giants...and we were like grasshoppers in our own sight, and so we were in their sight." (Numbers 14:1)

Notice the report "we were like grasshoppers *in our own sight...*" Someone once told me "Problems are what you see when you get your eyes off God's promises." The ten spies were like insects in their own sight – what they saw was without the direction of the Holy Spirit – and so they assumed they were similarly seen in the eyes of the inhabitants of the land.

"Leadership has never been about popularity"
(Sen. Marco Rubio)

A completely different viewpoint

The testimony given forty years later by their only ally in the city of Jericho, Rahab the harlot, gave a completely different viewpoint from the "we are grasshoppers" perspective. While the spies had concluded that they were nothing but insects to their enemies in Canaan, the Canaanites had made an opposite observation:

> "...the terror of you has fallen on us, and...all the inhabitants of the land are fainthearted because of you. For we have heard how the LORD dried up the water of the Red Sea for you when you came out of Egypt, and what you did to the two kings of the Amorites... whom you utterly destroyed...*as soon as we heard these things, our hearts melted; neither did there remain any more courage in anyone because of you, for the LORD your God, He is God in heaven above and on earth beneath.*" (Joshua 2:9-12 Italics added)

If only they had trusted their God! If they had followed their leader, Moses, when they first came to that border crossing, all of the people could have entered the land of promise. Everyone would have seen the glory of God. They all could have beheld Him, by His power, push aside the concerns, the cares and the fears that had gripped their hearts.

While studying one day a number of years ago, a Bible fact dawned on me – <u>Every miracle in the Bible begins with an impossible situation</u>! The God of the Bible is not daunted by the challenges facing us in this life. Not only is He *able* to meet every challenge on our behalf – He is *willing* to go before us to "vanquish" every enemy (Job 32:13).

An amazing outcome

Given the backdrop of historical human discontent, it is surprising that the leaders in Acts 6 were able, with relative directness and ease, to produce on their first attempt, a solution to their challenge that was immediately and widely accepted and embraced.

> "...<u>the saying pleased the whole multitude</u>. And they chose Stephen, a man full of faith and the Holy Spirit, and Philip, Prochorus, Nicanor, Timon, Parmenas, and Nicolas, a proselyte from Antioch, whom they set before the apostles; and when they had prayed, they laid hands on them." (Acts 6:5-6)

This is amazing! What started out with a "complaint" ends with consensus, agreement and contentment! It looks like everyone is in on board with the plan!

> "The congregation thought this was a great idea (so) they went ahead..." (The Message Bible, parenthesis added).

The passage is rendered in various translations with minute nuances in wording, but the message is always the same. Everybody is happy with the outcome. "The proposal" or "the idea" was put forward, accepted and acted upon. We never get the sense from the passage that this solution was "crammed down anyone's throat." It wasn't rammed through or forced on the people. It was presented and everybody began to nod their heads in agreement – "Yup, yeah, uh-huh, that's how I would've done it."

A "win" for everyone

A consensus was reached because it was a good idea and it met the objective. It was a "win" for everyone involved. The Hellenistic widows won because they were re-included in the daily distribution. The Apostles won because they got some much-needed help in the leadership and administration department. The new leaders won because they got recognized, promoted and had the chance to exercise their God-given gifts for the good of the whole group. And the church won because they now had an established "leadership path" and the administrative know-how to address future challenges as they would arise (you didn't think we'd get away with solving just one problem did you?).

"Leadership is solving problems"
(Gen. Colin Powell)

No longer isolated individuals...

Modern day pastor, prophetic voice and author Francis Chan has made the following observation:

> "Luke, the author of Acts, said that the early church was devoted to fellowship. The word fellowship sometimes has strange connotations in the church today. If it sounds cheesy, lighthearted or old-fashioned to you, then you have the wrong idea about fellowship. The first Christians shared their lives with one another. It wasn't about church picnics, potlucks or small talking in the "fellowship hall." They were real people meeting real needs and joining together to fulfill a real mission. They weren't meeting together because they kind of felt like they should. They shared their lives because in Christ they had everything in common. They truly loved each other. They cared deeply about God and His mission on earth, so they joined with the other Christians around them and worked together toward the (His) goal...Individualism is widely celebrated in our culture. We like to think of ourselves as self-sufficient and independent, able to "make it on our own." Sadly,

many Christians have adopted this individ-
ualistic mindset. Nobody is going to tell us
how to spend our time or our money or tell
us what to think. Sound familiar? ...One crucial aspect of submitting to Jesus is committing to the ministry of His church. We are no
longer isolated individuals, but members of
Christ's body."[27]

Is everybody happy?

The "saying pleased" the whole group. The Greek word
for "pleased" here means "to be agreeable or to seek to be
so"[28]. To seek to "be so" what? To want to be, to try to be,
to act like I'm – *agreeable*! To seek agreement with each
other. This could infer that not everyone was 100% on board
when the idea first surfaced. Maybe a few had their doubts
or there was some inner turmoil among the leaders and/
or the people. Maybe at first they didn't all see the value.
Perhaps a few folks didn't like change and voiced a dissenting
opinion. Things don't always go the way we think they ought
to but in the long run, as we stay open and connected with

---

[27] Chan, Francis (with Mark Beuving); "Multiply..."; David C. Cook,
Colorado Springs CO, 2012; pp.289-292

[28] Strong's Exhaustive Concordance of the Bible; Strong, James;
Hendrickson Pub. 1890, NT #700

the Lord and our fellow seekers, we find that He is in our midst and He is leading us into His victory.

Living a life of "gain"

The Apostle Paul exhorted his protégé Timothy:

"Godliness with contentment is great gain" (1Timothy 6:6)

NOT Godliness with grumbling. NOT Godliness with complaining or lamenting or accusing or grousing about how good the old ways were. Someone asked me "How many Christians does it take to change a light bulb?" OK, I give up—What's the punch line? "It takes six Christians to change a light bulb – one to change the bulb and five to stand around and talk about how good the old bulb was!" It would be funnier if it were less true!

"If you don't like change, you're going to
like irrelevance even less"
(Gen. Eric Shinseki, US Army Chief of Staff)

While not addressed in the narrative, one can't help but wonder if anyone among the widows raised a question. "Well, OK, but where's Peter? You know he always brings my daily portion personally; we've never done it this way before."

Some people refuse to be happy

Earlier I said this chapter was about the "ability to be content." In spite of the fact that some people refuse to be made happy, it seems that these leaders and people were able to come together seeking a solution. In the midst of the challenge they were able to be content. The "saying pleased the whole multitude" – whether immediately or eventually, the entire group found that a satisfactory solution had been discovered. And *that* is impressive!

A "vital connection"

As we close this section I'd like to point out something I call "the vital connection" between the leaders and the people. The leaders were ready to meet the need. It is equally noteworthy that the membership was ready to let them try without dictating the methods or the people involved. Someone once told me there are two reasons leadership fails: 1- Leaders who can't lead and 2- Followers who won't follow. Look at Paul's explanation of spiritual gifts to the Romans:

> "Having then gifts differing according to the grace that is given to us, let us use them: if prophecy, let us prophesy in proportion to our *faith*; or ministry, let us use it in our

ministering; he who teaches, in *teaching*; he
who exhorts, in *exhortation*; he who gives,
with *liberality*; he who leads, with *diligence*;
he who shows mercy, with *cheerfulness*."
(Romans 12:6-8 emphases added)

The Apostle isn't randomly preferring some gifts while
poking a finger at other gifts. He is neither endorsing nor
maligning those who operate in those gifts. Rather he is
deliberately mentioning the gifts he senses are at work in a
particular scenario. He then begins articulating not just their
existence, but the *way* in which each of the gifts should be
utilized. I've highlighted these usages with italics. The gifts
should be demonstrated in *faith*, in *ministering* (to others), in
teaching (an action and an activity), in *exhortation* (encouragement of others), with *liberality* (lots of it) and *cheerfulness* (joyful ease). All of this is given within the context that
the gifts are all deliberately "differing" (purposely different)
from one another. The "vital connection" then between the
leaders and the people comes down to the reality that it
is OK that there are many variables. Furthermore there is
a deep-seated confidence that those variations in people,
leaders and gifts are all working together for the higher good
of the whole organization. They are all assuming the best
about one another and they are certain that God is working
all in all (1Corinthians 12:6).

Are you Objective or Objectionable?

I would call Paul's approach an "Objective focus" as opposed to an "Objectionable focus". An objective focus is looking for answers while anticipating a positive outcome. An objectively focused person expects good things to happen, they just have to assess the situation and pursue the right "vein" of potential solutions. In other words, they anticipate contentment.

An objectionable focus is just what it sounds like – a focus that *objects* to its surroundings. It's the attorney in the courtroom who raises an "objection" every time the attention of the court is directed away from his preferred plan. The objectionable approach voices disagreement at every possible juncture and for every possible reason. While the objection may be a shrewd and useful court strategy, it is an unwelcome distraction when one is attempting to accomplish the tasks required for leadership, unity and agreement.

We have everything to rejoice about

Content-able people see beyond their own fears or concerns. Their focus is not solely upon their own comfort or convenience. They put their energy into growing instead of grumbling. As Christians we have everything to rejoice about and nothing to worry about – yet the discontented continue to raise their objections. In the story from Acts 6 the people and their leaders experienced a challenge, embraced it and grew together. Wouldn't you love to see this same outcome in your "group"?

"If you're saved, kindly inform your face"
(Dr. Joyce Meyer)

The point is, not only should we manifest the goodness, the glory and the power of God, but we should do it with a great attitude! We do God's will and we do it happy! God's gifts cause joy to well-up inside of us, they breed contentment in the inner depths of our hearts. We excel when we walk with Him. We are blessed as we obey His calling and His leading. Life is never more satisfying or fulfilling than when we live in His will and walk in His way. Contentment comes when we decide to live *our* life according to *God's* plan! The reason the saying pleased the whole multitude is that they found God's desired outcome for the future and they went with it!

Second Wind Principles

Read:

You will show me the path of life; In Your presence is fullness of joy; At Your right hand are pleasures ("agreeable, beautiful, pleasant, sweet" Strong's #5273 OT) forevermore. (Psalms 16:11)

Reflect:

I used to think God "lived" in the church and the rest of the time I was pretty much on my own. I never really thought the church was His literal house per se, but I lived as if my life had two spheres: Church and Everyplace else. His presence, fullness, pleasures are an everyday commodity – not things that get "rolled out" on Sundays or special meetings and then stored away until the next "big deal" at church. Our contentment is on-going. God is ever-present. Therefore, His gifts, His graces, His power, His presence, His goodness, His love and His provision are everyday "commodities." They are available to us at all times simply by inviting Him into the most common moments of our lives.

Reset:

1. When was the last time you were totally content, at rest and enfolded in His peace?

   _____

   _____

2. What if anything has disturbed the "fullness of joy" found in His presence?

   _____

3. What circumstances or people enhance or distract from your sense of peace?

_____

_____

4. What steps can you take today to refresh your sense of contentment and rest for the days ahead?

_____

_____

Chapter 9

CONTINUED BLESSING

Acts 6:7 "...the word of God spread...the disciples multiplied greatly..."

J esus highlighted the importance of firm foundations in
His Sermon on the Mount:

> "...whoever hears these sayings of Mine, and
> does them, I will liken him to a wise man who
> built his house on the rock...the rain descended,
> the floods came, and the winds blew and beat
> on that house; and it did not fall, for it was
> founded on the rock." (Matthew 7:24-27)

A strong and solid foundation supports a tough and resil-
ient structure. A weak underpinning yields a disastrous long-
term outcome in construction AND in life.

"Foundation stones"

The early chapters of the Book of Acts are the "foundation stones" for the rest of the New Testament. In fact, they are the underpinning and the superstructure for the Church as we know it today. In them we find the Ascension of Jesus to Heaven, the outpouring of the Holy Spirit on the early church and the beginning of Christians meeting from house to house. In these first chapters we find that all of the aspects of the ministry of Jesus (healing, deliverance and preaching) are still being carried out and being expanded by the disciples. The church is growing, leaders are being added, role-definition is being developed. The early chapters of the Book of Acts provided for the establishment of that historical group of believers as well as laying out the bulwark for the largest religious pursuit the world has ever known. The Christian Church was born!

God's blessing equates to growth

Biblically speaking, everything God blesses is growing. Flocks, herds, fields, individuals, groups, families, nations – all find themselves on the increase when they are built on the firm foundation of God's design. All will continue to grow as they pursue the purposes for which they are intended.

"...a great many (non-believing) priests were
obedient to the faith..." (Parenthesis added)

The foundation and the demonstration were so obvious, forceful and effective that even those who had expressed disdain for the movement found themselves convicted and convinced that they should get on board. The authority, the grace and the openness of this new pathway to God was intriguing and productive – many wanted a closer look!

"Hitting people over the head is assault not leadership"
(Pres. Dwight Eisenhower)

Two Disneylands

Prior to our entry into pastoral ministry, my wife and I lived in Southern California. This is significant because most of my family lived in the northeastern part of the country, and as a result we were continually entertaining out of state guests. Most everyone who visited wanted to go to Disneyland at some point during their stay. As a result of having been there numerous times, we knew Disneyland like the back of our hands – every ride, every shortcut, every angle for beating the lines at the rides and concessions. But there was a whole dimension of Disney that we knew nothing about.

There are really two Disneylands! Let me explain. The obvious Disneyland is the Magic Kingdom. The shops, the concessions, the shows, the parades, the Dumbo Ride – you get the picture. Everything you can see is in the first Disneyland. But then there is another "kingdom." It's the world behind the world of Disney. In this dimension, through a series of tunnels and hydraulic lines and back passages, run all the circuitry, controls and personnel that make the "magic" of the Magic Kingdom. In fact, the Disney we see could not even exist without the Disney hidden from view. A friend of mine has called it the "Disney parallel universe."

Parallel worlds

The "parallel effect" resident in Disneyland's "two worlds" can be related to the worlds surrounding humankind. We have the seen, known, felt, "natural" world and then we have the sensed but not seen, suspected but not really known, parallel world of the supernatural. There is a "God-world" behind our "real-world" (much discussion could be had around the subject of which world is more real – the natural or the supernatural – a subject for another time).

Paul reflects that we currently "see dimly but then (at some future time) clearly, face to face" (1 Corinthians 13:12 parenthesis added). There is a whole world going on behind the tangible setting of the everyday lives we lead. The allusion from Scripture is that this "parallel world" is the real driving force behind the things that we see personally, locally and globally. Writing to the Colossians Paul explains God's role in the "two world system":

> ...by Him all things were created that are in heaven and that are on earth, visible and invisible, whether thrones or dominions or principalities or powers. All things were created through Him and for Him. And He is before all things, and in Him all things consist. (Colossians 1:16-18)

It was all created in Him, by Him and for Him (John 1:3). We are both invited and welcome participants in the final act of the greatest "show" in the history of all the cosmos.

Irrespective of what we see, feel, know or what we think we see or feel or know – it is only in Him that we "live and move and have our being" (Acts 17:28). The church exists to give tangible, visible, experiential evidence to the goodness, love, power, activity and current-day reality of the Lord God Almighty. Because the church is from Him, for Him and all about Him – it is imperative that she continue in the same focus, freedom and function, by and for which she was established.

No spectators!

Church is not a spectator endeavor! It will never be passé, archaic or outdated. It was never intended that ministry should be left to the "clergy" (i.e. paid priesthood) while the "laity" passively sits on the sidelines hoping that somehow when the "pearly gates" are opened they can quietly and unobtrusively slip on in. Kenny Chesney, a modern-day country music performer sings the lyrics "everybody wants to go to heaven but nobody wants to go now!"[29] For the most part I'd say that is a true statement. But the timing of that heavenward journey notwithstanding, the fact remains that we all do want to go to heaven at some point. With that truth in mind it behooves us to know God's plan and what we can do to maintain the orthodoxy and the divine functionality of the church. For it alone is the Spirit-inspired "vehicle" intended to help us arrive safely in the eternal presence of our Almighty Father.

I thought I was "good to go"

I first came to the Lord at the tail of end of what has become known as "the Jesus Movement." I was much like those unbelieving priests in Acts 6:7 – I hadn't set out to seek God, find God, know God or pursue God. In fact, though I

---

[29] Chesney, Kenny: Song "Everyone wants to go to heaven"; From Album Lucky Old Sun; Blue Chair Records, 2008

was pretty sure there was a God, I had no interest or intent in getting close to Him. I thought if you went to church you were "good to go" and "don't bother me with all the details." But I had overlooked the "parallel universe factor!" I didn't know that God was motivating and mobilizing His intended bride to "come out from the unclean thing" (the world and its visible, human-kingdom ways) (1Corinthians 6:17 paraphrase). I didn't see that He was working behind the scenes. I didn't realize that He has a bigger plan in play and that we are all invited to be a part of His "end game." A major part of God's plan requires the continued effectiveness of His church. He, in turn, guarantees that He will bless her members both corporately and individually.

"Whatever you are – be a good one"
(Pres. Abraham Lincoln)

There are no accidents in God

The first portion of the Book of Acts clearly portrays the dynamics of God's plan to continually grow and bless His bride. From the beginning we see that healthy people will grow a healthy organization. All we really need to do is to seek His help and heed His direction. Some of the successes in the Bible seem to me to be accidental or incidental except that I know that there are no accidents in God.

How did they do it? There were no church-growth seminars, no leadership books, no Bible colleges or seminaries. There was God, His Holy Spirit and His people – and that seems to be enough for Him. There is an obvious sense of His blessing on that "formula" and upon the whole story. All things are working together; salvation, water baptism, deliverance, baptism in the Holy Spirit, people sharing the work, a good spirit, a can-do attitude, joy, excitement, inter-cooperation between members and leaders – signs of health and help and hard work are everywhere – Interestingly, when we get to the final verse of our study we find that we have come full circle:

Acts 6:7 "...the word of God spread...the number of disciples multiplied greatly...and a great many of the priests were obedient to the faith." Remember how the story started? Acts 6:1 "...the number of disciples was multiplying..." (Sounds like a repeat performance!)

Coming back bigger, better and stronger

In fact, we've come more than full circle because we did not arrive back at the beginning of our journey under the same conditions in which we left. We made our "circle" and came back bigger, better, stronger and with more adequately prepared leaders and members. We've been trained and tested. We've been through the fire and the flood and have been neither burned nor drowned (Isaiah 43:2) – in fact we are more inclined than ever not only to save ourselves, but to reach out a helping hand to others struggling with the same issues we've had to face.

In our lives as we walk with Him and abide by His commands we can expect: Expansion – Multiplication – Divine Insight–Challenge – Strength – Courage – Compassion – Continuous Growth – Change – Promise – Provision. Our study in Acts 6 has shown that all of these characteristics combine and work together for the good of those who are actively pursuing the furtherance, the growth and the active expression of God's holy kingdom on the earth in this day.

Second Wind Principles

Read:

"I am the Alpha and the Omega, the Beginning and the End," says the Lord, "who is and who was and who is to come, the Almighty." (Revelation 1:8)

Reflect:

The Book of Revelation is a reiteration by John the Apostle of the things that he saw, heard and experienced through an intense time of God's visitation during his imprisonment on the island of Patmos in the waning years of the 1st Century AD. At least four times in the book it is restated that the Lord is He "who is and who was and who is to come." My observation here is that I would not have placed the tenses of His presence in this order. I think the "normal" western order of thought would be a statement more like "He was, and is, and is to come." In our way of thinking we start in the past and "graduate" to the future. But God is deliberate – He states His first "point" first – "HE IS!" Sure He was and He will be but for us in our current day, in our right-now circumstance, the thing we really need to remember is that He Is! He is here, He is at work, He is always functional, He is always on our side, He is never going to let us down. To my way of thinking, *THAT* is the best news that any of us will ever hear spoken over our life, our possibilities or our destiny.

Reset:

1. Is there anything hindering you from seeing God as currently and mightily at work in your present circumstances?

   _____

2. Is there anything that you know needs to change in order for God's grace, approval and favor to be poured out right now (sin, negative habitual behavior, relationships)?

   _____

3. What step(s) can you take today toward realigning your life to begin moving toward your destiny?

_____

_____

Chapter 10

PUBLIC RECOGNITION

- Acts 6:6 "...they laid hands on them."

(The seven chosen men were) "set before the apostles; and when they had prayed, they laid hands on them." (Acts 6:6 parentheses added)

One of the greatest privileges of "Second Wind Living" is that we get to infuse others with the same energy and outlook that we have come to know. We get to encourage them with their own Second Wind. And here's the really great news: We don't have to wait until they're barely dragging themselves through life to minister to them. They don't need to be sitting on the sidelines with their tongue hanging out and gasping for breath. We can "pre-charge" them with the enthusiasm, the courage, the discipline and the determination to live in victory no matter how difficult the journey may become.

"What you make happen for others
God will make happen for you"
(Dr. Mike Brown)

Public affirmation is Biblical

We can open doors of excellence and opportunity by speaking into their lives with affirmation and support. The affirming process gets even more powerful when we have the chance to declare our positive belief in them and our anticipation of the awesome future that is awaiting them in front of their peers. There are powerful biblical examples of publicly affirming others, especially those we are raising to assume important levels of leadership.

Jesus Christ, at His baptism by John the Baptist, was publicly acclaimed by His Father in Heaven:

> "When He had been baptized, Jesus came up immediately from the water; and behold, the heavens were opened to Him, and He saw the Spirit of God descending like a dove and alighting upon Him. And suddenly a voice came from heaven, saying, 'This is My

beloved Son, in whom I am well pleased.'"
(Matthew 3:16-17)

The Gospel of Mark recounts the same event and makes the interaction even more personal with specific and direct affirmation saying "**You** are my beloved Son, in whom I am well pleased" (Mark 1:11 emphasis added). Even Jesus benefitted from the knowledge that His "Boss", the Father in Heaven believed in Him and supported Him in His work and in His authority.

Mark's gospel, later, at the Mount of Transfiguration reinforces that first acknowledgement of Jesus by recounting that when they were standing on that mountain "a cloud appeared and enveloped them, and a voice came from the cloud: "This is my Son, whom I love. Listen to him!" (Mark 9:8 NIV emphasis added). Not only are Son-ship and love reiterated but authority is reinforced and obedience is directed with the command – "Listen to Him."

The power of public affirmation

I can't help but wonder about the long term impact these moments had upon Jesus and His next several years of service, care, preaching and leadership. The Book of John recounts that at the last earthly meal He would share with His disciples:

"Jesus, **knowing** that <u>the Father had given all</u> <u>things into His hands</u>, and <u>that He had come</u> <u>from God</u> and <u>was going to God</u>, rose from supper and laid aside His garments, took a towel and girded Himself." (John 13:3-4 emphases added)

Jesus, about to face what were undoubtedly the most difficult hours of His earthly life, could reflect back and return in His mind to those days when He had heard from heaven – "I love You," "I believe in You," "I am with You." He was reinforced in His task. He knew He had the approval and the authority of the Father to continue forward. He knew He wasn't on His own and that the courage and strength He needed were at His disposal. John's account goes on to tell how Jesus, in those last moments "girded Himself" and continued to serve His friends and His associates. Undaunted. Unshaken. Unafraid. Powerful!

In my own life, I have had moments of affirmation from peers and overseers that have rested in my thinking and upon my heart to such a degree that I have been able to "feed" upon those interactions during future challenges. One such time was the occasion of my ordination as a minister in 1993. During that celebration I was surrounded by supporters—my wife and children and friends and family were there. My parents were both there. Several of my college professors were in attendance. The pastor of the church I attended during college conducted the service. There were executive leaders from the group of ministers to which I was being ordained. All of whom gathered around me, they laid hands on me, they spoke words of affirmation and positive reinforcement over me. In essence they all said – "We believe in you – you are loved."

I can do this!

The service lasted an hour or so, then everybody ate food and went home. End of story, right? Not quite. That service took place on a Sunday afternoon – but how many of you know what came next? Right – Monday! All of a sudden the party was over and it was time to go back to work. Stuff started happening. People showed up. Problems came along. Challenges in leadership and team-building emerged. "Life got real" as the saying goes.

There were days that I didn't think I could go on. There were times that I was attacked verbally or accused wrongly. Bad things were said. One guy even threatened to beat me up when he got the chance! At times I would say to myself – "This is ministry?" But I always came back to the times of affirmation – this wasn't my idea – this is God's plan. This is His way of securing the planet. The Lord's hand is at work IN me and THROUGH me – This is HIS idea and HE is bringing it to pass! He is empowering and affirming ME to do this not in my own strength but in His awesome and amazing power! I killed the lion, I killed the bear – Now bring on the big boy! For over twenty-five years I have continually reflected on God's call and the support of my peers and I have always come back to same conclusion: I CAN DO THIS! (And you can too!)

People need affirmation

As leaders, pastors, parents it is important that we recognize and remember that the people in our care want, need and deserve our recognition. The Acts narrative isn't satisfied to just share the seven names of the chosen, nor to stop with identifying their "job descriptions" (namely "serving tables" v. 2). Rather, the account verifies that all seven were publicly acknowledged for their leadership, godliness and reputation among the believers and within their community.

The Greek definition of "set before" demonstrates more than a call to the front of the room or a plaque or paper certificate printed by someone's computer! In the original language of the Bible, being set before the apostles carries the idea of "standing in" (the place of recognition) or standing by (suggesting a joining together with the apostles). Further exploration of the Greek reveals an appointment or a covenant with the seven. It means to establish, to present or to set in place.

"No one cares how much you know until
they know how much you care"
(Pres. Theodore Roosevelt)

Recognition produces enthusiasm

While in training in the Air Force it was not uncommon for the sergeant or the officer in charge to come before the flight (a group of several squads usually totaling about fifty to sixty service members) with a request – "I need five volunteers!" Of course, most of us were reluctant to volunteer because it usually meant that an unpleasant job needed some "grunt work" to be done and since we were the "grunts" – that meant that some of us were going to perform the distasteful task at hand. All of us, at some point, got to "pull the duty" and be the grunts for that day and for those particular tasks. The fact that grunts do grunt-work isn't really news to anyone. What I believe made these "volunteer" projects even more distasteful was that no matter how hard we worked or how many times we volunteered, no recognition was ever given. Now, I understand that we were being trained for war and that our Tactical Instructors (TI's) didn't need or want our approval. I can't help but wonder, though, if those airmen might have been more enthusiastic had they been occasionally recognized for their spirit and their performance.

Everyone wants their life to matter

Sadly, some companies, churches and even families approach their members much like those TI's treated us. They ask for volunteers. They require certain levels of commitment for membership. They expect specific areas of loyalty or performance. But they fail to recognize the positive attitudes, actions and accomplishments of those who faithfully commit to the group. Few aspects of life are more frustrating or more disempowering than the realization that the work in which we are engaged is un-meaningful or unimportant or will go unnoticed. Everyone wants to know that their life matters. We all want the sense that we are serving a cause higher, better, more powerful than our own private sphere. We want to know that we are having an impact that goes outside our own four walls and beyond our own personal existence.

...I trust you...

The "laying on of hands" is an old world custom seen from the beginning of recorded history. Leaders, fathers, elders, priests and government figures have always demonstrated favor toward their subordinates by touching them in some way. In our culture we shake hands. It's a greeting popularized during medieval times when most men carried swords. Since the majority of people are right handed, when someone offered to shake hands by extending their right hand, they were in essence saying "you can trust me and I trust you – and just to prove it I'm going to hinder my ability to draw my sword by obligating my right hand in an expression of friendship toward you." In our society, when someone graduates from a school or training program we affirm them by calling them forward and awarding them written and public acknowledgement in the form of a diploma. Many parents have chore charts or a system of stars, smiley faces or stickers for recognizing the children as they faithfully carry out the responsibilities that have been assigned to them.

Personal approval and future blessing

In the Old Testament a father laid hands upon a child to confer personal approval and future blessing. Kings, priests, prophets, judges and future leaders were publicly recognized by having hands laid upon them by those occupying roles of current leadership. Jesus laid hands upon the little children as a sign of His acceptance of them and His approval that they should remain close to Him and partake of His ministry, affirmation and love (Mark 10:13-16).

Dr. Jack Hayford in his commentary on Acts 6:6 makes this observation:

> Laying on of hands "is an act of ordination, a transferal of authority and responsibility, also indicating an acknowledgement of mutual identification and partnership with those commissioned to service"[30]

---

[30] Hayford, Dr. Jack; footnote re Acts 6:6 from Spirit Filled Life Study Bible p 163

Not only do we see the transfer of authority and responsibility, we bear witness that those who are so recognized are considered to be in "mutual identification and partnership" with those who are in leadership. This is a vital aspect and the completion of the "volunteer cycle" of identifying, calling, equipping and releasing those who are called to lead, serve or minister. As pointed out earlier, any leadership assignment not only has authority and responsibility but is held in check by and in submission to some level of accountability. This "communication loop" must, at some point, include those responsible for the recognition and promotion the individual.

Leadership is a function

Among the leaders at our church we have a saying: "Leadership is a function not a position." In any group there will be those who should be leading but are not. There will also be those who should not be leading but insist that they should be granted that authority. A friend of mine says of this dynamic – "If they really want to lead or if they really don't want to lead...they shouldn't lead." Why would he draw that conclusion? Because both reluctance and ambition can de-rail a person's leadership potential. If they really want a position they may be more focused upon themselves than upon the group and the purpose of the task/role at hand. If they really don't want to meet the day to day demands of leadership, they will most likely lack the diligence and the determination required to carry out those duties with excellence.

"What you do has greater impact than what you say"
(Stephen Covey)

Look for proven performance

Note! Don't make the mistake, like I did, of promoting someone based upon your perception of their long-term potential. What are you saying? Isn't potential what God looks at? Doesn't He look at the heart and not just the physically apparent? Yes! And therein lies His strength – He can see the heart clearly. The prophet Jeremiah observes that "the heart is desperately wicked" and wonders "...who can know it?" (Jeremiah 17:9) There are two who can "know the heart" – the Lord and the person who owns the heart in question. For everybody else, it's a guessing game. The only way we truly know what is in the heart is the guidance of the Lord and the long-term performance of the individual. Of course, I didn't know all this when I started out so I made plenty of mistakes and had more than my share of power-struggle situations when it came time to ask those involved to either "move up" or "move out." I remember one especially difficult fellow who had been a college friend of mine. It seemed as if he had a counter point to every point I raised. Every decision, every piece of the vision, every leadership activity had to be gotten past this guy – and he made it clear that he was not going to make that process easy for me. Eventually, he moved out of the area so I pretty much dodged the bullet, but I learned a lesson – take your time in placing people into key leadership roles. A friend of mine says it's easier to "elderize" someone than it is to "un-elderize" them. Bad English – Good statement – I learned it the hard way! Take your time in the placing of leaders – you'll be glad you did.

Lead by leading!

We won't rehash everything regarding leadership from earlier chapters but I will add this: When I look for leaders, I look for those who lead by leading! Profound, huh? Why do I look for people who already leading? Because LEADERSHIP IS A FUNCTION! I want to know: Who do the people look up to? Who are they following? Is that person an influence for the positive? The apostles wanted men of "good report" in the community. Why? Because those are the people the group will turn to when there is trouble or confusion or a problem to be solved. When I seek out leaders I'm looking for people who are influencers in the group. Let me be more clear and specific – I look for those who are a *positive influence* on the group. Did I really have to say that? Isn't it obvious that we want positive influence?

The Message version of the Bible translates Acts 6:3 this way: "...choose seven men...whom *everyone trusts, men full of the Holy Spirit and good sense"* (emphases added). I'm reading between the lines here, but I hear the writer saying "there are some people who are not trusted." In my experience, there are some untrustworthy people – even in the church! I write this section as a kind of balance between affirming everyone and recognizing that some people, once affirmed will attempt to use that leadership and that recognition to "ply their own trade" among the people in your group.

Complete confidence

The Apostle Paul wrote to his young protégé Timothy regarding this dynamic and its potentially deleterious effect upon specific individuals and the possible negative impact upon the group. In his letter Paul encourages a thorough "vetting" of sorts for any new leader. It is vitally important that we, as leaders, have complete confidence in the character, the judgment and the ability of anyone to whom we will extend privileges of authority – especially any role which involves the care and leadership of other people. Listen to Paul's advice to Timothy regarding those whom he will place over others:

> "He must not be a recent convert, or he may become conceited and fall under the same judgment as the devil (i.e. pride). He must also have a good reputation with outsiders, so that he will not fall into disgrace and into

225

the devil's trap." (1 Timothy 3:6-7 NIV parenthesis added)

The New King James Version cautions that the leader
candidate should not be a "novice" (a newcomer).

The New Living Translation is pretty clear in laying out
that the "...elder (leader) must not be a new Christian,
because he might be proud of being chosen so soon, and
the Devil will use that pride to make him fall. (1 Timothy 3:6
NLT parenthesis added). How about this rendering from the
Amplified Bible:

> He must not be a new convert, or he may
> [develop a beclouded and stupid state of
> mind] as the result of pride [be blinded by
> conceit, and] fall into the condemnation that
> the devil [once] did. (1 Timothy 3:6 AMP
> emphasis added)

I don't think it could be said much more clearly than that!
While we are all about encouragement and shared leadership
and the release of authority to associates in leadership, we
must also be aware and alert that, as Jesus cautioned, there
some who are "wolves in sheep's clothing" (Matthew 7:15).

A disproportionally strong effect

Years ago I came to the sobering realization that every group has members that influence for the good of the operation. And every organization harbors those who bring influence but have a doubtful, negative or undermining flavor that they express when sharing with others within their group. Here's the really sad part; sometimes those negative voices have a disproportionately strong influence upon the health and future potential of the organization.

I've discovered "prayer meetings" that gathered to discuss in negative terms their feelings regarding the vision of the church or my service as a congregational leader. One time I had a small group decide that I was actually a mouthpiece for evil and not leading people into godliness at all. The leader of this group once told their members that while in "prayer" for Deby and me she had "seen a red door." The apparition led her to conclude that we were leading people to hell with our lives and our teaching. I found it particularly amusing that while I had no knowledge of her "vision," within a day or two, Deby and I, as part of an ongoing household remodeling project, painted our front door red! You should have heard them go on about the "truth of the prophecy" of this woman. Here's the sobering part – this woman was in our church, she was a leader in our church (inherited from former leaders) and she was amazingly divisive and negative toward me, my family, my leadership and our church as a whole – the real kicker was that I hadn't known anything about it!

I once had two sisters attending our church who, while as friendly and seemingly godly as anyone we'd ever met; were secretly going around visiting people in the church trying to turn them against the vision and the destiny the Lord has laid out for us. They would tell people that they shouldn't tithe or the best way to influence the future direction of the church was to refuse to serve or volunteer or give. It's true, those things do hinder our work, but the more important issue to face is that people with these types of perspectives somehow find their way into places of influence and left unchecked they can cause an alarming level of upheaval in your group.

It's OK to like your leaders!

I remember a cliché bumper sticker from years ago. It said something like "Friends are people you like who like you right back." Can I take a little artist's license with that statement and put it in church leader context? "Elders and leaders are people you like, who like you right back!" Did you know that it's OK to ONLY have people in your circle of influence who are in favor of you, who believe in what you stand for and who are willing to be a catalyst for what you are attempting to do? I love my leaders and their families AND they love me, my wife and my family right back! We work together, we pray together, we serve together, some of us have wept together – we are in this TOGETHER!

I have been astounded over the years at the many interactions with pastors and church members who are suspicious of one another. Sometimes they distrust each other. Sometimes they actively and vocally disparage one another. And get this, they think that this mutual subversion is normal and acceptable! I once had an elder confess that in his opinion, his real job was to "balance me out," to act as a "check" for my forward-leaning leadership. In other words, while I'm stepping on the accelerator, he spends his time "riding the brake" to keep momentum from developing. God save us from this crazy thinking!

"When a wicked man rules the people groan"
(Proverbs 29:2)

Your leaders must respect you

If you have leaders whom you don't like or who actively and regularly make it clear that they don't like, respect or follow you – then you have some work to do. My first hope for you is that you can meet with any leader who has a negative perspective and that you can come to a mutual agreement to grow a healthier relationship and then deliberately pursue that objective together. If that isn't possible, the next thing to decide is – are you willing to put in the time, prayer, care and painful effort it's going to take to remove and replace anyone who is unwilling to become an ally in the work that God has set before you?

Brace yourself! Because when you resist and confront these types of folks, the "fur" can really start flying! Often times they have been in a place of privilege for years and they are used to getting their own way. I once counseled with a small country church that had a "lead elder" who had been in the church for more than 50 years! He was also the biggest giver in the group and his preferred method of "influence" was to withhold his giving until he got his way. As you can imagine, it was virtually impossible for the pastor to lead in this environment. Sad to say, it took years but eventually this man passed away and that icy grip of control was finally released. In a similar situation, a friend of mine once served in a church that had several people who attempted to control through financial and verbal means. I remember calling him one afternoon to see how things were going. Upon my inquiry he chuckled and said – "I think I'm about three funerals away from a revival!"

God will identify new leaders

I have to admit that I laughed at my friends' response, but really, could anything be more disappointing? In order for the will of God to be done, some of His precious saints must be laid to rest? It's a sad observation but one not without precedent. Isn't this precisely what happened when Moses led the children of Israel to the edge of the promised-land but they chose to follow a bogus and fearful report rather than the direction of Moses or the Lord? (Numbers 13:31-33) The result? A whole generation needed to wander in the desert for forty years until that group no longer had influence over the people. Then God raised up a new generation of leaders who were willing to follow His directions.

So what can we, as leaders, do when we come face to face with the realty of disgruntled, disenfranchised or dysfunctional leadership team members? Here are few ideas:

1. Set clear standards and expectations – The very first time I led a board meeting I entered the room thinking that I was in charge. It had never occurred to me that not everyone in the room was on-board with my leadership. Unbeknownst to me the board of that church had adopted, over time, the philosophy that everyone was, in essence, a leader of the meeting. In their estimation I was just another voice in the crowd. After listening to all kinds of banter and discussion I got the floor and set a standard. "I'm assuming that everyone in this meeting is a tither – if anyone is not a tither then by the time of our next meeting it is expected that everyone will either be tithing or they will no longer be a part of this meeting." Well, all I can say is it got real quiet all of a sudden. I had become the #1 buzz-kill of the church board meeting! By the

way, our next meeting had fewer than half as many in attendance as that first meeting!

2. Allow time for self "dis-inclusion" – The best way to move people around is to have them come away wanting the change that is set before them. When we set clear expectations we allow others to examine those parameters and decide whether this opportunity is a good fit for them. When I clarified that tithing was a minimum expectation of church board membership, several realized that this role was not a true calling for them.

3. Celebrate those who step up AND those who step down – This relates to the public recognition idea discussed earlier. Pointing out that someone has gained a level of leadership is important because it demonstrates to the group that we are "in covenant" and that we are standing together in this work. It gives them the conveyed authority to carry out the demands of the role they will be inhabiting. Likewise, when someone has completed their cycle or they have arrived at the conclusion that this role is not a good fit for them we should recognize them, thank them publicly, applaud them and bless them. This accomplishes a couple of things for the group. For one, it lets people see that it's OK to take some time off. Secondly it ends that person's season of service

on a high note and inclines them to be interested in serving again at a later date or in another capacity.

4. Continually "brag" about those who serve well – One time we had a situation where I went to pray for a man who subsequently died. Shortly thereafter a leader from our church went to pray for someone scheduled for surgery and the operation was canceled when the doctor observed that person was healed and no longer needed the treatment. A few weeks later I was teaching on leadership and operating in the authority of our calling. My focus was on the need to recognize the anointing resting upon those among us who are appointed to various levels of leadership. One issue that often comes up among church members is whether the Sr. Pastor should be visiting hospitals and homes to pray for the members. In some church settings this is a huge deal and a major part of the pastors' time, effort and ministry. During the course of that series I mentioned that I had prayed for a man who died, but Bob had prayed for a man who ended up not needing the scheduled surgery. I then followed up with a question: "The next time you're sick, who do you want to pray for you...Bob or me?" Everyone laughed and applauded Bob. The point is, others besides the senior leaders can pray and sometimes those prayers have surprising results! Exalting the positive and the excellent serves two

functions. First, the authority of those good leaders is highlighted and enhanced, causing people to want to be with them and follow them. Secondly, the contrast between those who are serving in unity with the leadership team and those who are "bringing a bad report" becomes ever-clearer so that the negative report is seen for what it is, down-played and ultimately ignored by the people.

The bottom line...

The bottom line is this – LEADERSHIP IS A FUNCTION NOT A POSITION! Never appoint anyone to a position unless you can clearly articulate their current function.[31] At the same time, once you have identified those who are functioning and serving and giving to the benefit of the whole organization, recognize them publicly. Lay hands on them. Publicly esteem their care and love and ability. Sing their praises. Brag on them in the staff meeting, at the church service or during your next leadership banquet. And then, when they decide it's time to move on or to take some down-time, celebrate that as well. Let everyone see that you are a healthy and safe and embracing group. Show the world that we don't

---

[31] For more specific details of the expectations placed upon leaders look at the apostle Paul's charges to Timothy and Titus (1Timothy 3:1-13; Titus 1:6-9, 2:1-10) See also 1Peter 5:1-9 for directions in orderly church leadership and membership.

just care about numbers or income, but that we have truly embraced the realization that the most important part of what we do is the care and nurture and recognition of the people who make up the group.

Second Wind Principles

Read:

"I have a special concern for you church (or business or household) leaders. I know what it's like to be a leader, in on Christ's sufferings as well as the coming glory. Here's my concern: that you care for God's flock with all the diligence of a shepherd. Not because you have to, but because you want to please God. Not calculating what you can get out of it, but acting spontaneously. Not bossily telling others what to do, but tenderly showing them the way... (Then God will see)...that you've done it right and commend you lavishly." (1Peter 5:1-4; The Message, parenthesis added)

Reflect:

The term "leader" implies "out in front." Someone has said that the leader must be far enough ahead to see the future but not so far out there that they lose sight of their followers. It's something of a precarious balance. Peter points out that out the primary test of leadership is not practical outworking or tangible success (though those things are important), but faithfulness to the cause – "the diligence of a shepherd." Our satisfaction in leadership comes not from what we personally get out of the role or its' leverage. True contentment as a leader is born out of the satisfaction that results from performing our calling with excellence before God and man. Part of being diligent to the call of God is our personal attitude and performance. Another part of diligence is faithfully identifying, equipping and empowering those who are destined to serve with us in the work of leading. Meaning well is good but well-meaning coupled with right-doing is even better! One might think of this as fine-tuning our leadership team.

Reset:

1. Many leadership coaches will say that you need to "Hire one person, Fire one person, Stop doing one thing and Start doing one thing"
   a. Do you need to release someone? Who? Why?

   _____

   b. Is there someone who can take your team to a new level? What do you need to do to recruit them to "your side"? _____

   c. What are you doing that someone else can do?

   _____

d. What do you need to begin to do to grow personally and/or organizationally?_____

_____

_____

2. What affirmation have you received that keeps you
going "on the inside"? How can you pass that reinforcement on to others? _____

_____

_____

3. Who can you acknowledge and encourage today?
(Hint: it's quite possible that this person is within
your own family or on your current team)

_____

_____

Chapter 11

THE JOURNEY CONTINUES

The Future is Bright – The Value of Vision

In a bizarre example of false piety Judas Iscariot chastised the disciples and Jesus by informing them that an alabaster jar full of perfume (Mark 14:5) should have "been sold and given to the poor" (John 12:5). One can't help but snicker at the parenthetical inclusion by the Apostle John that "this he said not because he cared for the poor but because he was a thief...and used to take the money from the money box" (John 12:6). Even Jesus had internal challenges in His team of world-changers!

The direction I take away from this exchange among the disciples is found in the answer that Jesus gave after affirming the priorities of the woman with the perfume. Encapsulated in the context of clarifying godly order in the anointing of Himself, Jesus makes the comment "the poor you will always have with you" (John 12:8). At first glance this could look as if

Jesus doesn't care about the poor. Or worse, He could actually be taking some sort of a "swipe" at the poverty-stricken. In making that assumption one misses the point of the correction brought by the Son of Man.

Our priorities come from God

In this instance the reference to the poor has less to do with poverty and poor people than it does with helping us to establish godly priorities for our lives. He's not saying "you'll always have the poor so just live with it." Jesus is pointing out that regardless of Judas' motives or Peter's future care for the "sheep" (John 21:7) or John's proximity to the Lord at the table (John 13:33) – the priorities of the Kingdom must always remain preeminent.

Wayne Cordeiro writes:

> "Peoples' needs are great and their expectations are endless. You cannot base your life and ministry on the expectations of others."[32]

Our service in the church and the care for the issues of the body are validated and directed by the Lord. Our priority system is drawn from the heart and the example of God Himself.

---

[32] Cordeiro, Wayne; "Leading on Empty"; Bethany House, 2009; p.193

Jesus in the passage is saying – "You will always have people trying to influence your values and your priorities, your role is one of service to Myself and My Father in Heaven – do not allow others with their own agenda, no matter how pious or righteous the motive may seem (i.e. – "given to the poor"), to superimpose their order of importance over Mine."

Our role in His Kingdom is to care and to love and to grow—these are His intended functions for our lives. As we obey and serve and expand the Kingdom, His will is carried out locally as well as on a grander scale in the world at large. His thinking and desire is NEVER shrinking but always growing. WE could call it "Excellence on the Increase" in God.

Excellence on the increase

Our Church Destiny Statement makes a bold proclamation:

"Celebrate! Family Church is a place of hope, health and restoration, a place where thousands of people from every cultural group gather to experience the love, the forgiveness and the healing power of God in a positive, relevant presentation. We are a big church with a close community feel."

The statement is especially bold because on a good Sunday we may see around 200 people in church, yet we declare we are serving "thousands"! Are we fooling ourselves or unable to count or are we just lying? Or...are we seeing beyond the natural, past the obvious, outside of our everyday experience? Our Destiny is not "pie in the sky" as some might suggest.

Destiny is an ultimate outworking. It is something down the road. Destiny is a promise, a preferred outcome – a dream in the making. Our Destiny is who we are becoming and what God has in store for us in the days ahead.

> *"Lean on, rely on and be confident in Him*
> *and He will bring it to pass"*
> (Psalm 37:5 – The Amplified Bible)

God's plan for you is bigger

The Scripture teaches that we serve the God "...who gives life to the dead and calls those things that do not exist as though they did..." (Romans 4:17). Every created thing did not exist just prior to the moment the Lord spoke it into being. Our God sees past the obvious or the already existent and builds His desired outcome through creative expectations and authoritative vocalization. He speaks...the world changes – pretty straight forward!

More than natural eyesight

When we look at life whether individually or corporately, we should look with an eye not limited by what is merely physically seen. Can we be bold enough and confident enough in the promises of God to look at life in terms of what can be or what should be or what could be? Your life, my life, the life and impact of the church is intended, in fact *Destined,* to be more and bigger and better than what we have seen thus far. Paul taught the Corinthian church "...Eye has not seen, nor ear heard, Nor have entered into the heart of man the things which God has prepared for those who love Him" (1 Corinthians 2:9). That's a pretty big statement! Whatever you can think or dream or imagine...God's plan for you is bigger!

At one point the Lord Himself told the prophet Habakkuk "I am working a work in your days which you would not believe, though it were told you" (Habbakuk 1:5). It's as if God is saying "You wouldn't believe it if I told you, so I'm going to have to show you." God is saying that same thing to His leaders and to His church in this day! The Lord and Creator of the universe is raising His voice and declaring to the world: "I am not done yet! Keep watching, I am about to blow your mind with my plan for your future"!

It's true, our Church Destiny Statement does make some pretty grandiose claims. That's because our God has shown us that we can believe Him for some pretty amazing provision!

You talk'in to me?

A few years ago I sensed the leading of the Lord to speak for a few weeks in church about the personal call of God. As my opening to the series I searched the internet and found about ten applications of the now-famous Robert DeNiro line from the 1976 movie "Taxi Driver". At one point in the movie DeNiro looks in the mirror and provocatively asks several times, "You talk'in to me?" My point was that many of us have forgotten that God is, in fact, talking to us! I wanted to express the reality that God has particular "thoughts" that He thinks about each one of us (Jeremiah 29:11). Each of us has a calling and it rests with each one of us to "reason together" (Isaiah 1:18) with the Lord to draw conclusions as to how we should live in light of that prescribed future He has in mind for us. The New Living Translation cites Isaiah 1:18 this way "...let us argue this out..." The admonition is not one of a shouting match with the Almighty, rather it is an invitation to listen to (His) reasoning and to allow Him to make His case for His ability, His power and His love for us. God is expressing His desire to see us succeed.

Keep your head in the game

This discussion prompts me to ask some questions of the reader. What are you looking at? Where is your focus? What do you expect or anticipate from your life, from your Lord, for your future? Our local track coach shouts to the runners on the field, "Don't look back, the race is in front of you!" A life-lesson can be learned from that statement: Keep your head in the game and your "eyes on the prize" no matter what is going on around you.

David Allen calls this principle, "Applied Outcome Thinking" (AOT). Simply put, AOT is the

> "discipline of identifying the real results you want and, more specifically the projects (or actions) you need to define in order to produce them." In its most basic terms it is defining what we expect to see, accomplish, produce or enhance with the application of a chosen action. It is prefaced by and incorporated into a process of self-revelation using questions (such as):

"What do we want to happen in this meeting?"
"Why do we use this form?"
"What would the ideal person for this job be able to do?"
"What do we hope to accomplish with this software?"
"Why are we doing this?"
"What are we trying to accomplish?"
"How will we know when we succeed?"

Outcome focusing leads us to base our meetings, decisions and actions upon specific desired ends that result from our current and future input and effort."[33]

A place in God's amazing plan

Mr. Allen calls it AOT, the Apostle Paul said "I press on, that I may lay hold of *that* for which Christ Jesus has also laid hold of me" (Philippians 3:12 Italics added). I personally believe that God has a *"that"* for every person, for every business, for every church or mission endeavor. *THAT* simply put, is the purpose – the singular aspect of life or business or ministry or care – that only you or your group can bring to the fore. You have a specific, God-honoring, value-producing, life-changing calling that is unique to your gifts and your group. It's actually quite exciting to think that each of us is so valuable and so important to the Lord that we have been granted a place at His grand "staff meeting" of world-altering personalities.

Whether you are called to pastor or counsel or coach or teach or manage a business or manage a household – Do you still have your eyes on the goal? Are you still engaged? A man in his mid-70's recently told me "I quit going to doctors about 30 years ago". Curiosity got the best of me, "Why", I asked. He smiled as he answered "Because they always

---

[33] Allen, David; "Getting things done…"; Penguin Publishing; New York NY; 2001; Chapter 13

found something wrong with me." He continued, "I stopped going 30 years ago and I haven't been sick a day since!" What would you say this man is looking at? Aches? Pains? Problems? Worries? Nope! It seems to me that he is thinking ahead. I'll bet he's looking at the future. Not just any generic future either – He's looking at HIS future! I'm pretty sure he's not worrying about everything that could go wrong either. I'm willing to bet he's focused on the day, the week, the year, the life in front of him. He's still in the game! And he's planning to keep moving forward! Almost 80 years old and still looking ahead – now THAT'S what I'm talkin' about!

"I can make it through anything..."
(Philippians 4:13 – The Message)

The value of vision

We can simplify the expression of Destiny and Vision by saying that vision will give us <u>Direction</u>, <u>Correction</u> and <u>Connection</u>:

Direction

- An instructor of mine said "If you're going nowhere, any road will take you there" – Your destiny is the road map to your future – Direction defines the journey.

Correction

- A written Destiny Statement acts as a guide to keep me accountable and causes me to ask myself, "Have I gotten off-track anywhere?" Correction keeps us on the road.

Connection

- The vision helps me to keep moving or to start again if I have stalled; and then it helps me measure my progress – Connection guides our action to accomplish our goals.

Destiny and vision will keep our head and our heart in the game.

God can do anything

The Apostle Paul in his letter to the Ephesians lays out his long-term vision for his friends:

> "My response is to get down on my knees before the Father, this magnificent Father who parcels out all heaven and earth. I ask Him to strengthen you by His Spirit – not brute strength but a glorious inner strength

– that Christ will live in you as you open the door to invite Him in. And I ask with both feet firmly planted on Love, that you'll be able to take in with all the Christians the extravagant dimensions of Christ's Love. Reach out and experience the breadth! Test its length! Plumb its depths! Rise to its Heights! Live full lives, full in the fullness of God.

God can do anything you know – far more than you could ever imagine or guess or request in your wildest dreams! He does it not by pushing us around but by working within us, His Spirit deeply and gently within us." (Ephesians 3:14-21a "The Message Bible")

One final word

This book has been about leadership – but it's more than that. Leadership is fundamentally about relationship – so this is really a story of people and how they learned to relate to one another. Even more than that, it's a road map to guide us into better, stronger, happier, more productive relationships in our own respective worlds.

Prepare to be blessed

We must continually remind ourselves: All big things in Scripture happen in the midst of extreme turmoil and while experiencing significant challenge. Every biblical miracle is brought about by impossible circumstances! We are in good company when we think that we are out of options and the problems far outweigh the promises and the possibilities. It is during our most challenging times that our Great God will do His best work. If you are in a time of struggle right now I have good news YOUR LIFE IS NORMAL! What you really need at this time is a SECOND WIND! Prepare to be blessed by God. Please join me on a wonder-filled journey. May His peace and His joy be yours, today and always.

Second Wind Principles

Read:

"Love has been perfected among us in this: that we may have boldness in the day of judgment; because as He is, so are we in this world." (1 John 4:17)

Reflect:

The "boldness" touted here is in the same vein as "the right to become children of God" offered in John 1:12 for those "who believe in His name." It's not arrogance to walk in the power, the presence or the privilege He has granted to His own. In fact, just the opposite, it is ignorance and denial to insist on living at a level below that for which He has sacrificed to attain our status as "heirs of God" and "joint heirs with Christ" (Romans 8:17). We are His righteousness (2 Corinthians 5:21) and intended to live in the grace, the power, the love, the blessings and the favor of Creations' Heavenly Father! Notice one final thing, the emphasis on life in His presence is not "on-hold" until we get to heaven...It is to be embraced and lived right now "in THIS world!"

Reset:

1. Say this: "I resolve today to walk, talk, live and believe according to the victory and the calling that God has appointed for me."
2. Now, say this: "I will not apologize for, nor avoid the anointing or the advancement he has pronounced over my life as His child and His heir."
3. What is hindering your ability or your *availability* to be "as He is...in THIS world?" Will you renounce it, avoid it or quit it today? _____
4. Pray this: "This day Lord I believe and receive You as my Lord and Savior – I will live my life with you from this day forward. Thank you for forgiving me and for saving me. Amen."

Appendix I:

CHURCH STRUCTURE

The "stuff" never rolls uphill!

I' ve never really liked the classic "pyramid-model" for flow charts that articulate and diagram corporate or governmental structure. They're all essentially the same. The Chief Executive Officer (CEO) is at the top. Next, there's a line or two of other executive involvement, a Chief Operations Officer (COO) and/or a Chief Financial Officer (CFO). Then comes the "middle management" with a few branches, maybe some Vice-Presidents of this and that. There could be some pecking order lined out for ranking the folks in the middle. And then, of course, there's everybody else. I've always looked at those from the bottom up thinking "OK when the stuff starts rolling (and it never rolls uphill) who's at the bottom of this pile? And, who is going to get dumped on the worst when the stuff hits the fan?" Call me cynical or call me realistic – I'm just sayin'!

I prefer an atomic model

Because of my dislike for the aforementioned, we came up with what we think is a better graphic for demonstrating corporate structure. Our diagram can't really do our system justice because when using a printed page, we are essentially limited to two dimensions – Length and Width. Nevertheless, the idea can be communicated. Notice that the diagram is circular and pretty much flat as opposed to a pyramid. We are deliberately trying to demonstrate that this isn't intended to be a portrayal of personal value but a picture of corporate function.

In my mind's eye I see this diagram more like the atomic models we had in sixth grade science class. Those models showed the relationship between the nucleus, the protons, the neutrons and the electrons not by their intrinsic value to the structure but according to their placement within the structure. In truth, no one element of the atom is more or less important than another because if any of the parts are absent or fail to function the entire atom is negatively impacted.

Each of us plays a key role

Our purpose for the "atomic structure" diagram is to demonstrate how each of us plays a key role in the makeup of the whole of the church. It is a visual portrayal of Paul's first letter to the church at Corinth in which he points out "the manifestation of the Spirit is given to each one for the profit of all...one and the same Spirit works all these things, distributing to each one individually as He wills" (1 Corinthians 12:7, 11).

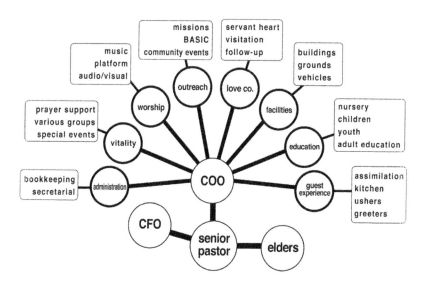

Appendix II:

CHURCH COMMUNICATION

Clarify the vision

A common mistake of leaders is failing to recognize that although the vision is clear in our minds, it may not be as apparent in the thinking of our constituency. We assume that people know what we are talking about. We often throw around colloquialisms, acrostics and abbreviations as if we expect them to be everyday jargon for everyone in our organization. The actual truth is that we, as leaders, are pretty much the only ones who think like this.

I can't even begin to tell you the number of times I have been excitedly powering ahead with some explanation or future plan only to stop for a breath (finally!), look around and find that half the group is doodling on their folders while I'm pretty sure the other half haven't even heard a word I've said – Cue the crickets!

A leader must communicate

It was during a meeting like this that I sensed the Lord waking me up to a reality – If I want the people to be on board with the vision and our future, then the incumbency is upon ME to see that they are fully up to speed and that they understand all that we are attempting to communicate. That was when the Lord showed me a picture in my mind of what we have come to know as "Concentric Rings of Influence".

When I first came to the church the focus for the previous few years had been re-establishing and stabilizing the congregation. It had been a rough stretch of years prior to my arrival. I was the twelfth pastor the church had seen in seventeen years of existence. Because of the massive turnover in previous leadership the people were uncertain and some were even suspicious of the "new kid" who had arrived on the scene. A few even mentioned that they were there before I got there and they would be there when I left. One dear saintly lady, after I had served the church for a little over a year informed me that "if" I lasted another six months then I'd be the longest term pastor they'd ever had! It was that little word "if" that had me concerned...What were they planning to do me in the next six months anyway?

Everyone wants a positive future

The "Concentric Rings" graphic is a tool that I constantly review in my mind. Because the church had struggled just to keep the doors open for so long, there had been very little emphasis on vision or destiny or any long-term plan for the future. Everyone was still trying to decide if the church even *had* a future! As we moved forward we got healthier. We grew numerically and spiritually. We began to trust one another. We started to believe there was not only a future but a divine destiny awaiting us and we began identifying and articulating what that future would look like.

We crafted vision and mission statements. We created standards for and a clear path to pursue "official" membership. We established Biblical eldership as the leadership model we would employ for the day to day care, nurture, protection and promotion of the church. We gained traction, we built momentum, we continued to grow. As we grew we found that communication became more difficult, more cumbersome and more complicated. It seemed there was just no way to get all the information out to all the people for all the events and opportunities that were presenting themselves.

Information is constantly moving

And that's how the "Concentric Rings" came into being. We had to find a way to get all of the people on board for all that was going on. We found that since, statistically, 30% of the church will be gone on any given Sunday, a pulpit or bulletin announcement would always miss at least a third of the people and we never knew which third that would be. Additionally, as I mentioned earlier, bulk announcements are our least effective communication and recruitment tools anyway. We needed to be able to continually communicate outwardly from the center of our decision-making body to reach even those who attend nominally or infrequently.

As you look at the Concentric Rings you will see that the information is constantly being disseminated from the pastors, elders and staff outwardly toward the farthest reaches of the congregation. The process is continually working in reverse as well – with details streaming toward the center from the periphery.

Communication takes many forms

We employ all kinds of methods for getting the word out. The church Facebook page gets a lot of attention. Written bulletins are published once per month (this has saved a ton in copy expense and office prep time). Pre and Post-service media slides depicting coming events and announcements are shown on the screens in the sanctuary, in the hallways, in the café and in the children's ministry rooms. We do use pulpit announcements but we are always aware of their potential for ineffectiveness. We also use word of mouth, posters and emails. The youth group and its leaders favor "text blasts" (announcements sent to many cell phones all at once) as their preferred method of information sharing.

We inform our key people first

Take note of one important factor – we make sure to inform our key people BEFORE we make any bulk announcements! This is demonstrated by their location on the inner rings of the circle and illustrated by the arrow moving progressively toward the outer rings of the diagram. Our core leaders are among the first to hear about coming events or changes. Likewise, they are the first ones offered the opportunity to speak into the process of deciding which information will be disseminated. This step is vital because there are few things more annoying to our leaders than to hear of some big news at the same time everyone else in the church is being informed. It makes them feel like they have no idea what is going on – because in fact, they have not been informed of what is going on!

The value of "buy-in"

Other values added by the employment of the Concentric Rings have been the dynamics of buy-in and momentum. Before any public announcement is made most of our leaders have already been made aware of the news being discussed. Since they have had prior opportunity to voice their opinions and express their ideas, the leaders by and large have already committed positively to the information before it is publicly released. The result of this endorsement and support is that as an announcement is being made or a plan is being revealed, there are numerous heads around the room or in the sanctuary already nodding in agreement. They are smiling and eager and high-fiving each other and that enthusiasm is contagious.

A quick segue here regarding the dissemination of information. A friend of mine says one of the most effective ways of moving information is to release the info to a few talkative individuals with instructions that they shouldn't tell anyone, the result being that in no time at all half the people in the church will have heard the selected announcement! Gossip, admittedly, is not a good thing; it seems though, that my friend has learned to turn even "loose lips" to the service of the Kingdom!

Unity is "good and pleasant"

The result of the "Rings" has been that we have virtually no public dissent, discord or disagreement because everyone who has leadership influence has already had the chance to have their ideas or concerns addressed and satisfied. It truly is "good and pleasant when brothers and sisters dwell together in unity" (Psalms 133:1) and good communication is a big part of making that dynamic of agreement a reality for the organizations we lead.

The "Concentric Rings of Influence"

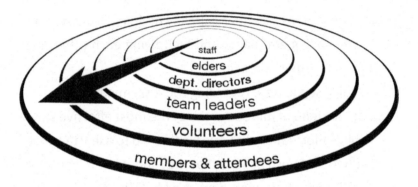

Appendix III

SEEKING PERSONAL REALIGNMENT

Considerations during a season of self-assessment:

1. What is my original call from God?
   a. Has it changed?
   b. Is it still valid and "in-play?"
   c. Do I need to be spiritually / ministerially "re-invented?"
2. What are the activities that I am involved in that I love the most?
   a. Be honest – not what is expected of me, but what do I like?
3. What activities and people drain my tank?
   a. Remember it's OK to have elders & members you like, who like you back!

4. If I retired today with several million dollars and no debts – what would I do?
    a. What makes you want to get out of bed every day?
    b. What excites you?
    c. When is the last time that you know for sure that you heard from God?
5. What triggered my depletion?
    a. When did you notice that your tank was running dry?
    b. What is causing your sense of burnout?
6. What am I doing now that I just can't do anymore?
7. What do I sense I need to begin doing?
8. What things do I enjoy doing but cannot continue to do to the level I am currently involved?
    a. John 15:2 "…every branch that bears fruit He prunes"
    b. Some good things may have to go to make room for the true assignment
9. With whom do I need to share / counsel so that the rebuilding of my life may begin?

BIBLIOGRAPHY

Allen, David; "Getting Things Done – The Art of Stress-free Productivity"; New York NY: The Penguin Group Publishing 2001

Barclay, William; "The Acts of the Apostles"; Philadelphia PA: Westminster Press 1976; pp50-54

Barna, George and Pastoral Care Inc. (Statistics); The Fuller Institute; Pasadena CA; 2015

Brown, Dr. Michael; Strength and Wisdom Ministries; Branson MO: 2005

Brown, Joel; 50 Inspirational John Maxwell Quotes; "Addicted2Success.com": Sept 2015

Bukofzer, Manfred F; The New Oxford History of Music 3: Oxford University Press, 1960

Chan, Francis (with Mark Beuving); "Multiply – Disciples Making Disciples"; Colorado Springs CO: David C. Cook 2012

Cordeiro, Wayne; Leading on Empty (Refilling your tank and renewing your passion) Grand Rapids, MI: Bethany House, 2009

Covey, Steven M.R. with Rebecca R. Merrill; "The Speed of Trust – The one thing that changes everything"; New York, NY: Free Press (Division of Simon & Schuster) 2006

Enlow, Johnny; "The Seven Mountain Prophecy – Unveiling the Coming Elijah Revolution" Lake Mary, FL: Creation House 2008

Hayford, Jack W. (General Editor); "The Spirit Filled Life Bible", New King James Version (NKJV); Nashville TN: Thomas Nelson Publishers 1991

Hillman, Os; "Change Agent – Engaging your passion to be the one who makes a difference"; Lake Mary, FL: Charisma House, 2011

Hsieh, Tony (CEO Zappos.com) "Delivering Happiness...A Path to Profits, Passion and Purpose" New York, NY: Hachette Book Group, 2010

Hvistendahl, Mara; "LENOVO" An Interview with Yang Yuanqing CEO of Lenovo (recently named #1 in global PC sales) from Delta Sky Magazine January 2016, pp 59-61

Hybels, Bill; "Leadership Axioms"; Grand Rapids, MI: Zondervan 2008

Johnson, Bill; Wallnau, Lance et al "Invading Babylon – The 7 Mountain Mandate"; Shippensburg PA: Destiny Image Pub. 2013

Lockman Foundation, The; "The Amplified Bible", Expanded Edition; LaHabra CA: Zondervan 1987

London, H.B. Jr. and Neil B. Wiseman; "Pastors at Greater Risk"; Ventura, CA: Regal Books, 2003

Maxwell, John C; "The 21 Irrefutable Laws of Leadership"; Nashville TN: Nelson Publishing; 1998

Osteen, Joel; "I Declare – 31 Promises to Speak Over Your Life"; New York, NY: FaithWords, 2013

Peterson, Eugene H.; "The Message – the bible in Contemporary Language"; Colorado Springs, CO: NavPress Publishing Group 2005

Semerda, Ernest W; "Medlert" CTO/Co-Founder; Twitter: @ ernestsemerda or Google: 2015

Siegel, Joel; "Assembled Together – The power of the local church"; Castle Rock CO: Big God Media / Siegel Ministries Inc: 2014

Strong, Dr. James; Strong's Exhaustive Concordance of the Bible; Hendrickson Pub; 1890

Swenson, Richard A. M.D.; "Margin"; Colorado Springs CO: Navpress; 1992

The New International Version (NIV); Biblica International; Zondervan Publishing; 1973

The New Living Translation (NLT); Tyndale House Foundation; 1996

Wigglesworth, Smith; Daily Devotional; New Kensington PA: Whitaker House; 1999

Welcome home
to
Celebrate! Family Church

The next time you are in the Leicester, NY, area please consider visiting one of our weekly services, or watch us online. Visit *icelebrate.org* for live stream, service times, special events, conferences, additional resources, and more.

If there is any way I can help you, your church, or your team, please get in touch. I'd be happy to serve you.

Be blessed in His presence today!
Dr. Eric W. Scott

RESOURCES by Dr. ERIC
for
FURTHER GROWTH
To order, visit *leadertoleader.net*

NEW BOOK COMING SOON!

"GOING VERTICAL"—When we align with God's plan - when we go vertical - we live "on earth as it is in heaven" - How exciting and liberating! This is Kingdom-now living! This book expands the *Going Vertical* audio message series by adding action steps, notes, plus many more details, references and application highlights.

AUDIO MESSAGES (on flash drive)

"GOING VERTICAL"—This groundbreaking 15-part audio series will teach you how to live earthly life in heavenly perspective, promise and power… to go vertical! This series was taught at Dr. Eric's church, and those who heard it are still talking about the radical transformation that took place by applying these principles of God's Word to their daily lives.

"STIRRED NOT SHAKEN"—Like the cool action hero of the silver screen who conquers perilous dangers, a Christian can move forward with confidence. This series walks you through I and II Corinthians, and teaches you to be stirred by the Spirit, but NOT broken, beaten or destroyed by life's challenges!

"EXPANSION DONE RIGHT—TIMING & LAUNCHING A START UP"—A single session presented to a group of pastors and leaders, this teaching is packed with practical and hard-won insights on planning and surviving the difficult first stages of a new work. Topics include: building concensus, developing a core of partners, raising up new leaders, making in-course adjustments, and more. A digital study guide is included.

"FACETS of FINANCIAL FREEDOM"—There's more to God's plan for your prosperity than throwing a few dollars in the offering plate next Sunday. Filled with solid Bible teaching, this 3-message series will change your thinking and change your life.

PERSONAL COACHING

Dr. Eric is available to encourage and help your church or business overcome the challenges you're facing. Whether through dynamic seminars, preaching, staff and leader training, or through personal assessment, together we will:

► Enhance and expand your vision
► Engage your God-given destiny at a new level of determination
► Experience the excellence of an empowered and confident Kingdom-now connection

CONTACT

You can contact Dr. Eric directly via:

✉ Email: *pastoreric@frontiernet.net*

f Facebook: *Eric W. Scott*

Got a bike? Let's ride. Get in touch with me and let's catch a little wind together. ∼*Eric*

CPSIA information can be obtained
at www.ICGtesting.com
Printed in the USA
BVOW08s0717220417
481752BV00003B/6/P